EDITOR: LEE JOHNSON

OSPREY
MILITARY

MEN-AT-ARMS 294

BRITISH FORCES IN THE WEST INDIES 1793-1815

Text by
RENÉ CHARTRAND
Colour plates by
PAUL CHAPPELL

First published in Great Britain in 1996 by
Osprey, an imprint of Reed Consumer Books Ltd.
Michelin House, 81 Fulham Road,
London SW3 6RB
and Auckland, Melbourne, Singapore and Toronto

ISBN 1 85532 600 0

Filmset in Great Britain by KDI, Newton le Willows
Printed through World Print Ltd, Hong Kong

Dedication

This West Indian study is dedicated to a fine old school I
attended many years ago: Queen's College in Nassau,
Bahamas.

Acknowledgements

We gratefully acknowledge the assistance given by Charles
Bradley, William Y. Carman, Don Crandall (Montserrat),
Randolph Jones, Philip Haythornthwaite, Douglas Hendry,
Vincent K. Hubbard (Nevis), Gaylord T.M. Kelshall
(Trinidad), Glenn Steppler, Don Troiani, Peter Harrington
of the Anne S.K. Brown Military Collection at Brown
University, the Library of the Royal Canadian Military
Institute, the Hougthon Library at Harvard University,
the Library of Congress, the University of Ottawa Library,
the Canadian War Museum, the National Army Museum.

Publisher's Note

Readers may wish to study this title in conjunction with the
following Osprey publications:

MAA 285 *King George's Army (1)*
MAA 289 *King George's Army (2)*
MAA 292 *King George's Army (3)*

Artist's note

Readers may care to note that the original paintings from
which the colour plates in this book were prepared are
available for private sale. All reproduction copyright
whatsoever is retained by the publisher. All enquiries
should be addressed to:

Paul Chappell
c/o 14 Downlands
Walmer
Deal
Kent CT14 7XA

The publishers regret that they can enter into no correspon-
dence upon this matter.

If you would like to receive more information about
Osprey Military books, The Osprey Messenger is a regular
newsletter which contains articles, new title information
and special offers. To join free of charge
please write to:

**Osprey Military Messenger,
PO Box 5, Rushden,
Northants NN10 6YX**

INTRODUCTION

Two centuries ago, the West Indies were a booming set of islands where vast fortunes were made. Sugar was the source of this wealth. To this was added other crops, much smaller but highly valuable, such as indigo and coffee. The British West Indies accounted for about one-fifth of Britain's foreign trade in 1789. This increased to a third during the 1790s.

By the late 1790s, the West Indies attracted four-fifths of British overseas capital investments and provided over one-eighth of the government's £31.5 million total net revenue to the Treasury through various direct taxes and duties. Considerable indirect tax income, perhaps another eighth, was generated from the West Indian commercial and trade activity. These figures explain the tremendous numbers of naval and military forces deployed to protect these valuable Caribbean territories.

Britain used its naval superiority and basically adopted the doctrine of overwhelming force to protect its investments by conquering the enemy's colonies. In spite of some setbacks in the 1790s, this strategy worked against smaller enemy islands. However, against larger islands, naval superiority and numerous regiments did not insure any success. After being repulsed by the Spanish in Puerto Rico, the British forces refrained from attacking large colonies.

Dozens of regiments served in the West Indies. Between 1793 and 1801, some 69 line infantry regiments were sent there. Another 24 followed between 1803 and 1815. The death toll due to tropical diseases was very high for European troops. From 1793 to 1802, an estimated 45,000 British soldiers died in the West Indies, including about 1,500 officers, nearly all from fevers. In 1796 alone, some 41 per cent of the white soldiers died, most of them having arrived within the past year.

In the following years, efforts were made to keep white troops out of unhealthy garrisons. As a result, the mortality rate dropped to 15 per cent in 1800 and remained at about 14 per cent from 1803 to 1815. Nevertheless, about 20,000 men

Part of the seaward battery of Fort Berkeley, one of several guarding the entrance of the important Royal Navy base at English Harbour, Antigua.

This small battery at Bransby Point, Montserrat, is typical of the many that dotted the coasts of most islands for protection against privateers and pirates. They were armed with older cannon of various origins served by militiamen and often by a few full-time 'mattrosses' hired by the local legislatures.

died from fevers, including about 500 officers.

The improvement in overall statistics was due, most of all, to the creation of regiments of black soldiers who were far less liable to deadly tropical diseases. By 1803, the proportion of black soldiers was about one to every two white soldiers in garrison. Generally, a force of at least 20,000 regulars, white and black, was considered necessary to keep the British West Indies secure.

CHRONOLOGY

Abbreviations: Bn= Battalion; Bns= Battalions; coy= company; coys= companies; Ft= Foot, regiment of; det= detachement; LD= Light Dragoons; LI= Light Infantry; R= Royal; RA= Royal Artillery; RIA= Royal Irish Artillery; RM= Royal Marines; RMA= Royal Military Artificiers; Vols= Volunteers; WIR= West India Regiment.

1 February 1793 – Great Britain, Spain, Holland, Sardinia, Naples and Portugal join Austria and Prussia already at war with France.

15 April – Capture of Tobago from the French: RA, RM, 9 Ft (Light coy), 60 Ft.

September (to December 1798) – British intervention in Saint-Domingue (or 'San Domingo' as the British call it), then a French colony, today called Haiti): RA, RMA, Dutch Emigrant Artillery (2 coys), 13 LD, 14 LD, 17 LD, 18 LD, 1 Ft, 13 Ft, 16 Ft det, 17 Ft, 20 Ft, 22 Ft, 23 Ft, 32 Ft, 35 Ft, 39 Ft, 40 Ft, 41 Ft, 49 Ft, 56 Ft, 60 Ft, 62 Ft det, 66 Ft, 67 Ft, 69 Ft, 81 Ft, 82 Ft, 83 Ft (3 coys), 93 Ft (det), 96 Ft, 99 Ft det, 130 Ft (Flank coys), 2 & 3 Irish Brigade Regiments, Bouillé's Uhlans britanniques, Hompesch's Hussars, Rohan's Hussars, York Hussars, 3 WIR, 5 WIR, 7 WIR. For local units (see the part on 'Saint-Domingue (Haiti)' below).

6 February – 23 March 1794 – Capture of Martinique from the French: RA, RIA, RMA, LD det (from 7, 11, 15, 16 LD), 6Ft, 8 Ft (Flank coys), 9 Ft (Flank Coys), 12 Ft (Flank coys), 15 Ft, 17 Ft (Flank coys), 22 Ft (Flank coys), 23 Ft (Flank coys), 34 Ft (Flank coys), 38 Ft (Flank coys), 39 Ft, 43 Ft, 56 Ft, 58 Ft, 60 Ft (Flank coys), 63 Ft, 64 Ft, 65 Ft (Light coy), 70 Ft, Carolina Corps.

2 April – Capture of St. Lucia from the French: RA, RIA, RMA, 6 Ft, 8 Ft (Flank coys), 9 Ft (Flank coys), 12 Ft (Flank coys), 17 Ft (Flank coys), 22 Ft (Flank coys), 23 Ft (Flank coys), 34 Ft (Flank coys), 38 Ft (Flank Coys), 43 Ft, 60 Ft (Flank coys), 63 Ft, 65 Ft (Light coy), Carolina Corps.

11 April – 10 December – Capture from and

loss of Guadeloupe to the French: RA, RIA, RMA, 8 Ft (Flank coys), 12 Ft (Flank coys), 17 Ft (Flank coys), 22 Ft (Flank coys), 23 Ft (Flank coys), 34 Ft (Flank coys), 38 Ft (Flank coys), 39 Ft, 43 Ft, 56 Ft (3 coys), 60 Ft (Flank coys), 63 Ft, 65 Ft (Light coy), Carolina Corps.

January 1795 – Holland is overrun by French armies and becomes the Batavian Republic, ally of France.

March – June 1796 – Carib uprising on St. Vincent: RA, RIA, 3 Ft, 9 Ft (Flank coys), 40 Ft det, 42 Ft, 46 Ft, 60 Ft, 61 Ft, 68 Ft (Flank coys), 2 WIR, Hardy's York Fusiliers, Lowenstein's Chasseurs, Ramsay's York Rangers, St. Vincent Rangers, Malcolm's Royal Rangers, Carolina Corps, St. Vincent Militia.

March – June 1796 – Fédon's Rebellion on Grenada: 17 LD det, RA, RIA, 3 Ft det, 8 Ft det, 10 Ft, 25 Ft, 29 Ft, 38 Ft, 57 Ft, 63 Ft det, 88 Ft, Royal Étranger, Carolina Corps, Malcolm's Royal Rangers, Grenada Loyal Black Rangers, Brender's Black coy, Grenada Militia.

Map of the West Indies. (Courtesy Francis Back)

April – 18 June – British lose St. Lucia to the French: RA, 9 Ft (Flank coys), 61 Ft, 68 Ft (Flank coys), Malcom's Royal Rangers.

8-17 June – French raid on Dominica repulsed: 15 Ft, 21 Ft, Dominica Militia.

July 22 – Spain and Prussia cease hostilities with France.

August – March 1796 – Maroon's rebellion in Jamaica: 13 LD det, 14 LD det, 17 LD det (two dismounted and especially trained troops), 18 LD det, 20 LD, RA, 16 Ft, 62 Ft, 83 Ft, Cuban Chasseurs, Jamaica Militia.

December – French raid on Martinique repulsed: 2 Ft, Black Rangers, Martinique Militia.

22 April – 2 May 1796 – Surrender of Demerara, Berbice and Essequibo by the Dutch: RA, RIA, 39 Ft, 93 Ft, 99 Ft.

26 April – 26 May – Recapture of St. Lucia from French: RA, RIA, RMA, 14 Ft, 27 Ft, 31 Ft, 42 Ft, 44 Ft, 48 Ft, 53 Ft, 55 Ft, 57 Ft, 2 WIR, Hardy's York Fusiliers, Lowenstein's Chasseurs, Ramsay's York Rangers, Royal Étranger, Malcolm's Royal Rangers, O'Meara's Rangers.

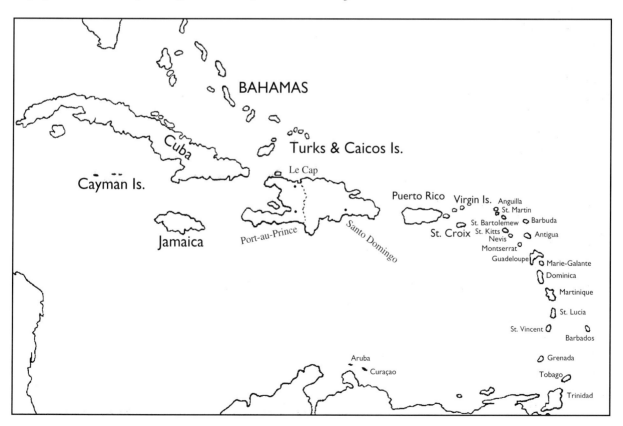

British troops besieging Fort Louis, Martinique, in March 1794. The two infantrymen at left wear red single-breasted jackets with black or blue collars and cuffs and white wings, white gaiter-trousers and visored caps with a bearskin crest. The two gunners next to them wear plain round hats, blue single-breasted jackets with red collars and cuffs and yellow wings, white pantaloons with short black gaiters. The three artillery officers at the centre wear the same dress but their coatees have short or long tails. To the right are two scarlet-coated infantry officers on foot wearing round hats, one officer having the light infantry wings and short tails, talking to a mounted general, possibly meant to be Sir Charles Grey. At the right, a mounted trooper from the Light Dragoons detachments wearing the Tarleton helmet and a blue jacket. Detail from an aquatint after a drawing taken on the spot by the Rev. Cooper Willyams. (Anne S.K. Brown Military Collection, Brown University, Providence)

June – March 1797 – Guerrilla warfare in St. Lucia: 31 Ft, 44 Ft, 48 Ft, 55 Ft, Ramsay's York Rangers, O'Meara's Rangers, Druault's Guadeloupe Rangers.

7 October – Spain at war against Great Britain.

27 November – French attack on Anguilla repulsed: Anguilla Militia.

17 February, 1797 – Capture of Trinidad from the Spanish: RA, RIA, RMA, 2 Ft, 3 Ft (Flank coys), 14 Ft, 38 Ft det, 53 Ft, 50 Ft det, Hompesch's LI, Lowenstein's Chasseurs, Soter's Royal Island Rangers.

18 April – 1 May – British repulsed at San Juan, Puerto Rico by the Spanish: 26 LD det, RA, RMA, 14 Ft, 42 Ft det, 53 Ft, 60 Ft det, 87 Ft, Lowenstein's Fusiliers and Chasseurs, Tobago Corps of Blacks.

27 April – British frigate *Experiment* raids fort and spikes guns at Truxillo (New Spain): RM, 42 Ft det, 53 Ft det, Irish Brigade det.

December – British naval raids on coast of Spanish Venezuela: Trinidad Rangers det.

June – October 1798 – Suppression of banditry in Trelawny mountains, Jamaica: 3 coys of embodied local woodsmen, Accompong Maroons.

3–10 September – Defence of British Honduras against Spanish at St. George's Cay near Belize: RA, 63 Ft det, 6 WIR det, local white and black vols and sailors.

20 August 1799 – Surrender of Surinam to the Dutch: RA, RIA, RMA, 60 Ft.

September 1800 – Surrender of Curaçao to the Dutch.

20 March 1801 – Capture of St. Bartholomew from the Swedish: RA, 3 Ft, 11 Ft, 8 WIR.

24 March – 1 April – Capture of St. Martin from the Dutch and French, and St. Thomas, St.

John and St. Croix from the Danish: RA, RIA, RMA, 1 Ft, 3 Ft, 11 Ft, 64 Ft, 2 WIR, 8 WIR.

12 October – Cessation of hostilities between France and her allies and Great Britain.

27 March 1802 – Peace treaty of Amiens concluded. All occupied overseas territories occupied by the British to be handed back except for Trinidad and Ceylon.

16 May 1803 – Great Britain declares war on France and Holland.

22 June – Capture of St. Lucia from the French: RA, RMA, 1 Ft, 64 Ft, 68 Ft, 3 WIR, Black Pioneers.

30 June – Surrender of Tobago by the French: RA, RMA, 1 Ft, 64 Ft, 3 WIR, Black Pioneers.

20 September – Surrender of Demerara and Essequebo by the Dutch: RA, RMA, 3 Ft det, 7 Ft det, 64 Ft, WIR det.

January 1804 – British raid on Curaçao repulsed by Dutch.

27 April – 5 May – Capture of Surinam from the Dutch: RA, R Foreign Artillery det, RMA, 16 Ft, 64 Ft, Rifle coy of 2 bn 60 Ft, 6 WIR, Black Pioneers det.

12 December – Britain at war with Spain.

22–27 February 1805 – Defence of Dominica: RA, 46 Ft, 1 WIR, Dominica Militia, Barbados Militia det.

March – French raids on St. Kitts, Nevis and Montserrat.

July 1806 – French raid on Montserrat. Raid on St. Kitts fought off by RA, 11 Ft, 70 Ft and St. Kitts Militia.

1 January 1807 – Capture of Curaçao from the Dutch: RM.

1 May – Abolition of slave trade in the British Empire.

September – British raid on Baracoa, Cuba, repulsed by Spanish: RM, 96 Ft (det).

21–25 December – Surrender of St. John, St Thomas and St Croix by the Danish: RA, RMA, 15 Ft det, 46 Ft det, 60 Ft, 70 Ft (Flank coys), 1 WIR det, 3 WIR (Flank coys), Black Pioneers det.

2 & 30 March 1808 – Capture of Marie-Galante and La Désirade from the French: RM.

May – Napoleon displaces the Spanish Bourbon royal family and installs his brother Joseph as king of Spain. Insurrections break out against French

Hardy's York Fusiliers, composed of Germans raised by Major T.C. Hardy, served at St. Lucia from 1795 until they were incorporated into the 3rd Battalion, 60th Foot in early 1797. They wore a black cap with brown fur, green jacket with black collar and cuffs piped red, red piping, brass buttons, red waistcoat and green pantaloons. (Anne S.K. Brown Military Collection, Brown University, Providence)

troops. Spaniards and the Spanish colonies remain loyal to the Bourbons and become allies of Great Britain.

4 July – British raid repulsed at St. Martin's by French and Dutch: RM.

19 August – 3 September – Relief of Marie-Galante: RM, 1 WIR (3 coys).

14 January 1809 – Capture of French Guyana: RM and Portuguese colonial troops from Brazil.

30 January – 24 February – Capture of Martinique from the French: RA, RA Drivers, R Foreign Artillery det, RMA, 7 Ft, 8 Ft, 13 Ft, 15 Ft, 23 Ft, 25 Ft (Flank coys), 60 Ft, 63 Ft, 90 Ft, 1 WIR, 4 WIR, 8 WIR (3 coys), Royal York Rangers, York LI Vols.

14–17 April – Capture of The Saints from the French: RA, RMA, 15 Ft det, 60 Ft, 3 WIR, 8

Ramsay's York Rangers. Often called York Chasseurs, this émigré unit was raised in 1793 by Capt. G.W. Ramsay and sent to St. Lucia and St. Vincent during 1796 and later was at St. Kitt's and Dominica. In October 1797, it was incorporated into the 3rd Battalion, 60th Foot and the Foreign Artillery. They wore a black cap with brown fur and a white metal star, blue jacket with yellow collar, cuffs and lapels, white metal buttons, yellow shoulder straps, blue wings with white lace, blue waistcoat braided white, and blue pantaloons. (Anne S.K. Brown Military Collection, Brown University, Providence)

WIR det, York LI Vols, Royal York Rangers (Flank coys).

7 July – Capture of city of Santo Domingo (now in the Dominican Republic) held by the French: detachments from RA, R Foreign Artillery det, 18 Ft, 54 Ft, 55 Ft, 60 Ft, 2 WIR, 7 WIR, Puerto Rico Spanish colonial regiment, Santo Domingo Spanish volunteers and militias.

28 January – 6 February 1810 – Capture of Guadeloupe from the French: RA, RMA, 13 Ft det, 15 Ft, 25 Ft, 63 Ft det, 90 Ft, 1 WIR (Light coy) 2 WIR (Light coy), 3 WIR (Light coy), 4 WIR, 6 WIR, 8 WIR, Royal West India Rangers, Royal York Rangers, York LI Vols.

15 & 21 February – Surrender of St. Martin's

and St. Eustatius by the French and Dutch: RA, RMA, 25 Ft, 4 WIR (1 coy).

6 April 1814 – Napoleon abdicates as Emperor of the French and goes into exile at Elba. Hostilities cease.

1 March 1815 – Napoleon's return to France provokes war with Great Britain and her allies. Defeated by the Duke of Wellington at Waterloo on June 18, he abdicates four days later and is exiled to the British island colony of St. Helena in the South Atlantic.

9–10 August – Capture of Guadeloupe, which had rallied to Napoleon: RA, 15 Ft, 25 Ft, 63 Ft, Royal West India Rangers, Royal York Rangers, York Chasseurs.

BRITISH ARMY WEST INDIAN DRESS

The uniforms of 18th-century British troops were hardly suitable for the tropics, but there were few attempts to adapt them. The only concession was the use of linen trousers in the West Indies instead of breeches and long gaiters during the 1780s. Various suggestions were made to adopt more suitable items such as round hats, of white or black felt, and, in 1791, infantry recruits for West and East Indies were issued a round hat, a sleeved red jacket with regimental buttons and collar, cuffs and shoulder straps in the facing colour and a pair of gaiter-trousers. These items were to be worn until the recruits joined their regiment. However, thousands of soldiers also reached the West Indies wearing much the same dress as they would in Europe, with predictable effect, as medical officers would soon report.

Improvements were sought and, in May 1795, soldiers going to serve in the West Indies were to have the following kit: 'a round hat as is furnished to recruits on foreign service, a plain red jacket so made to button close to the body and to have a stand up collar, under flannel waistcoat and drawers of the same [flannel], a pair of woollen trousers to button over the shoes like a gaiter, 2 shirts, 2 pairs of flannel socks, 1 black leather stock, 1 knapsack or pack.' In the autumn of 1795, a medical board further recommended that the tens of thousands of soldiers sent with Sir Ralph Abercrombie have round hats, the regimental coats with the tails shortened and Russia duck gaiter-trousers. Later, the 1802 regulations noted that, in the West Indies, the coats of sergeants and men were the same as in Europe, but without lining, and that they also had a pair of white linen trousers instead of breeches and long gaiters. On 7 July 1810, a circular ordered corps serving in West Indies to have gaiter-trousers of blue serge instead of white duck or linen. Highlanders posted in the West Indies were to have similar tropical clothing instead of kilts and trews. The undress consisted of a white round jacket with collar and cuffs of the regimental facing colour, white pantaloons and short gaiters.

From 1800, the hats were replaced by the regulation 'stovepipe' shakos and there appears to have been no peculiar model for troops in the tropics. The 'Belgic' shako, introduced in 1812, had a special model for troops in the tropics made of white felt, but this experiment was a failure. On 12 October 1813, a circular announced that the white shakos furnished for infantry in the East and West Indies were liable to damage from mildew and moths and would be discontinued and replaced by the standard shakos of black felt.

Throughout the period, officers, who were supposed to wear bicorns and long-tailed coats on duty, had their own unofficial order of dress in the West Indies besides the regulation uniform. This consisted of round hats and short-tailed jackets with white linen pantaloons and boots or half-boots.

For cavalry too, service in the West Indies brought about changes. The 20th Jamaica Light Dragoons used light-weight camblet cloaks which were officially approved for all cavalry in January 1796 as 'much lighter, & better Calculated to turn Rain' while the helmets 'should be made of Tin & lined with White linen' (WO 3/28). And on 30, September 1796, light dragoons in the West Indies were instructed to wear blue pantaloons.

Regimental distinctions for colonial units are

Lowenstein's Chasseurs or Legion, raised in Germany during 1795 and sent to the West Indies early in 1796. Drafted into the 5th (Rifle) Battalion, 60th Foot in June 1799. Black round hat with yellow cockade loop on the upturned side and a green plume, blue-grey jacket with green collar, cuffs, lapels and turnbacks, brass buttons, white breeches, black gaiters and armed with a rifle. (Anne S.K. Brown Military Collection, Brown University, Providence)

given elsewhere in this book; those for numbered line regiments will be found in Brian Fosten's *Wellington's Infantry* (MAA 114 and 119).

SAINT-DOMINGUE (HAITI)

The outbreak of the French Revolution soon brought political crisis to the French colony of Saint-Domingue (now Haiti), often called 'San Domingo' by the British and at that time the world's most prosperous colony. Order gradually collapsed and, in August 1791, the bickering between various factions of whites, free blacks and mulattos paled as tens of thousands of black slaves rose in a vast revolt which laid waste to scores of

Rohan's Hussars, an émigré corps raised in 1794 as two regiments amalgamated into one and sent to Haiti at the end of 1795. Devastated by fevers, the remnants were incorporated into the York Hussars in late 1797. They wore a black visorless shako with white plume and yellow cords, white pelisse with black fur and yellow cords, blue dolman with red collar and cuffs and yellow cords, blue breeches and blue sabretache trimmed yellow, blue valise trimmed yellow, white sheepskin over the saddle. (Anne S.K. Brown Military Collection, Brown University, Providence)

plantations. Planter families and their servants were often massacred with unspeakable cruelty. The local assemblies, overwhelmed by the gravity of the revolt, eventually appealed for help to the governor of Jamaica. Some assemblymen even went so far as to wear black British cockades. In September 1793, a British force arrived heralding five of the most tragic years in British military annals. Initially the intervention went well; after eight months and about 50 casualties, the British controlled about one third of Saint-Domingue with their headquarters in Port au Prince.

Many French royalist colonists embraced the British cause and vied to raise auxiliary colonial corps. General Sir Adam Williamson, British governor and commander-in-chief at Saint-Domingue, accepted many offers, perhaps too many. By the end of 1795, about 40 corps of various types existed. The Prince of Wales Regiment, the Royal Legion of Saint-Marc, the York Cavalry and the *Maréchaussée* (a militarised constabulary force) were mostly composed of free blacks. Generally, 'Chasseurs' and 'Volunteer' units consisted almost entirely of drafted slaves with white officers. Most localities also had militias which were paid and supplied when on active duty. In December 1795, the colonial forces amounted to some 11,000 of which about 4,000 were militiamen. The cost of it all to the British Treasury became horrendous, reaching as much as £700,000 a month!

There were many reasons for this. Colonels were allowed to purchase clothing in the West Indies, which was far more costly than procurement in England. Some corps listed fictitious men. The *Légion du Sud*, also called *Légion de la Couronne*, before its disbandment, was found to actually have only 31 officers and men. It was something of a family unit as all of them were related to one another.

A few officers at Saint-Marc even had commissions in three or four units. Meanwhile in Môle Saint-Nicolas, the Marquis de Contades' *Gendarmes royaux anglais* – a unit loosely inspired by the Gendarmes of the French royal guard and, no doubt, wearing its scarlet uniforms laced with silver – was, for a time, paid above the British rate and had double the required number of officers. The snobbish Gendarmes even formented a rebellion in early 1795, but were not disbanded.

At the same time, about 23,000 British and foreign troops in British pay poured into Haiti. Over three out of five died from malaria and yellow fever. Most British troops served in cities but the war in Haiti consisted mostly of countryside ambushes where, in spite of the good service of black chasseurs, the enormous amounts of money spent and the many regiments sent from Europe, the leader of the rebelling slaves, Toussaint L'Ouverture slowly gained the advantage.

In 1796-1797, General John Simcoe reduced the number of units to cut costs and reorganised the forces, but it was too late. His successor, General Maintland, faced a desperate situation. In March 1798, when the defence line of Arcahaye collapsed, the British were forced to evacuate Saint-Marc and Port au Prince in May to Jérémie and Môle Saint-Nicolas. From there the British forces, including many black soldiers, were evacuated to Jamaica during the summer and autumn. The disastrous British intervention had cost about 14,000 officers and men and a king's ransom.

The main units raised during the British intervention were as follows:

Dillon's Regiment

When the British arrived at Môle Saint-Nicolas in September 1793, the 2nd Battalion of the 87th French line infantry regiment (formerly Dillon's Irish) was in garrison, much weakened by sickness and demoralised by French revolutionary politics. Under the influence of Major O'Farrel, the battalion surrendered and most of its officers and men joined the British service forming a small corps of about 180 under its original name of 'Dillon'. It gave very good service, notably being 'firm as a rock' repulsing the enemy attack on Saint-Marc in

Hompesch's Light Infantry, also called Fusiliers and Chasseurs. Recruited in Germany during 1796, the regiment arrived in Martinique over 900 strong early in 1797, participated in the capture of Trinidad where it was left in garrison until December when sent to Antigua. In April 1798, its 545 officers and men were incorporated into the 2nd and 5th battalions, 60th Foot. Round hat with red turban, bearskin crest and green plume, green jacket with red collar, cuffs, lapels and turnbacks, pewter buttons, white waistcoat, green pantaloons piped red, armed with rifles. (Anne S.K. Brown Military Collection, Brown University, Providence)

Hompesch's Hussars. Raised in Germany during 1794, the regiment was sent to Haiti in early 1796 over a thousand strong but lost 90 per cent to fevers and ceased to exist in October 1797. They wore a red visorless shako with white plume and cords, green pelisse with black fur and white cords, green dolman with red collar and cuffs and white cords, red breeches and sabretache trimmed with white, green housings edged red and white, green valise edged red. (Anne S.K. Brown Military Collection, Brown University, Providence)

September 1794, but its numbers were constantly shrinking due to casualties and sickness. Only 58 were left by August 1795 and, while some recruits raised the unit to 106 by November, it dwindled out of existence during 1796. The 11 remaining officers were sent to other units that November. The uniform was a red coat with red collar, yellow lapels and cuffs, white turnbacks, brass buttons, white waistcoat. In Haiti, it had round hats, white pantaloons and short white gaiters.

Jean Kina's Corps/Chasseurs de George III.

In 1792, the white planters of Tiburon decided to arm some of their best slaves into a unit com-

York Hussars. Raised in 1794 from Germans, the regiment was taken on the British establishment and sent to Haiti, 680 strong, arriving in the spring of 1796. It gave service but a year later, less than 240 had survived the fevers. Other units were drafted into it bringing the strength up. It was evacuated to Jamaica in 1798, sent to England a year later and disbanded in July 1802. They wore a black visorless shako with white cord and plume, green pelisse with black fur and white cords, red dolman with green cuffs and collar and white cords, red breeches and valise laced white. (Anne S.K. Brown Military Collection, Brown University, Providence)

manded by the ablest of them: Jean Kina. It was soon the terror of revolted slaves hiding in the nearby mountains, its usual strength around 200 men. When the British arrived at Les Irois, in late 1793, they came into contact with Kina's Corps, already renowned for its successes in 'bush fighting warfare'. Captain Colville reported in October that the corps' appearance was 'supposed very grotesque – instead of Drums and Fifes they used Banger and Coromante flute, the musical instruments of their native country. Some had firearms, others bill hooks fastened to long poles and plantation watchmen's hangers and were generally attired in their osnaburgh frocks.' Kina's Corps was taken into British pay, issued with clothing and arms, deployed against the French black Republican forces and captured Tiburon in February 1794. It was part of the garrison of Tiburon in December when its fort was besieged

and bombarded. When a shell exploded in the trench where Kina's men were huddling, panic spread and 450 men fled out of the fort heading for the hills but fell into an ambush near Les Irois – where 300 were killed – the worst British disaster of their five years in Haiti.

The remnants of the corps were then posted at Port au Prince, and were eventually reorganised as *Chasseurs de George III* made up of two compa-

Bouillé's Uhlans britanniques. They were formed by Marquis Louis de Bouillé in November 1793, this émigré cavalry corps, which was composed mostly of Germans, was sent to Haiti in early 1796. On 27 August, its four companies were ordered to be incorporated into Montalembert's Légion britanniques de Saint-Domingue. They wore a white lancer cap with black fur, yellow cords and red plume, red jacket with green collar, cuffs and turnbacks, yellow braid, brass buttons, green waistcoat and trousers laced yellow, green housings and valise edged red, white sheepskin, yellow and red lance pennant. (Anne S.K. Brown Military Collection, Brown University, Providence)

nies. In June 1797, it carried out a successful attack on the outposts of Léogane. In the summer of 1798, it had 185 officers and men at Môle Saint-Nicolas, many of whom were evacuated to Jamaica with their commander on 1 October 1798.

Légion de la Grande Anse

Raised among white colonists and possibly some free mulattos in south-western Haiti from 11 September 1793 by the Canadian-born baron Jean-Charles de Montalembert to support the British troops, it had twelve infantry companies, two artillery companies and a cavalry detachment. It numbered about a thousand men. The legion, one of the most dependable and best disciplined of the early local units in British service, was in many actions, including the capture of Port au Prince and the defence of Léogane in 1794, where it served with distinction. In early 1795, it formed the basis of Montalembert's new *Légion britannique de Saint-Domingue*.

Dessource's Volunteers or Legion

Raised in late 1793 in the Saint-Marc area by Claude Bruno Dessource, a former officer in the Port au Prince French colonial regiment, Dessource's Volunteers consisted of slaves with white officers divided into ten companies of infantry, two of dragoons and one of artillery. It gave outstanding service in many engagements, notably in repulsing the attack on Saint-Marc's on 14/15 April 1795. It 'performed to the admiration of the whole garrison' and the corps was awarded a pair of colours by General Williamson. It was evacuated to Jamaica in August 1798.

Légion d'York

Not to be confused with the York Hussars, this unit was raised at L'Arcahaye, Haiti, in early 1794 by Jean-Baptiste Lapointe, mayor and commander of the town's National Guard (a ruthless local dictator promoted general by the British). The Guard, recruited from free blacks and mulattos, formed the nucleus of this corps. By December 1795, it was a mounted unit, the Duke of York's Cavalry Regiment, of about 240 officers and men. By June 1797, it was a legion consisting of a dra-

La Tour's **Royal Étranger** *or Royal Foreigners, over 1,000 strong, was sent to St. Lucia and Grenada in early 1796 and incorporated at Grenada and Barbados into the 60th Foot and the Foreign Artillery in February 1798. Grenadiers had fur caps with white plume and cords, fusiliers a bicorn, blue coatee with red collar, black lapels and cuffs, white lace, pewter buttons, white waistcoat and blue breeches. Round hat, no lace and white breeches on service in the West Indies. (C.C.P. Lawson after C.H. Smith sketches,* **Journal of the Society for Army Historical Research,** *1944)*

goon regiment of 327 officers and men divided into five troops with some auxiliary infantry and artillery. It was a well-disciplined unit and was involved in many victorious engagements. Most officers and men appear to have evacuated to Jamaica with Lapointe in 1798. The unit was said to have worn the 'scarlet uniform of the British'. By regulations of 25 June 1797, colonial dragoons had a uniform jacket, a Russia duck stable jacket,

Buttons of émigré units found in Grenada. At left a brass button, probably for an officer and once silvered, of **Royal Étranger.** *Crown over RE and the émigré's motto:* **TOUJOURS FIDELES AU ROI** *(Always faithful to the king). At centre a brass button with RL, for* **Royal Liègois,** *renamed* **Royal Étranger** *in late 1795. At right, a pewter button of Prince Salm Kybourg's regiment which was drafted into* **Royal Étranger.** *(Don Troiani collection)*

cloth pantaloons, a hat or helmet, half boots, a large cloak, shirts, socks, shoes and a stock.

Légion britannique de Saint-Domingue (Montalembert's)

Authorised raised in British regular service on 9 December 1794 as the *Chasseurs britanniques de Saint-Domingue*, it consisted of ten infantry and two artillery companies, amounting to some 1200 officers and men. Under the command of Baron de Montalembert, it incorporated the *Légion de la Grande Anse* in Haiti and recruits from Europe. In December 1795, Charmilly's *Ulhans britanniques de Saint-Domingue* were incorporated into this unit. In June 1796, the corps was re-organised as a legion with ten companies of infantry, six of cavalry and two of artillery, and renamed *Légion britannique de Saint-Domingue*. On 27 August 1796, Bouillé's *Ulhan britanniques*, a four-company corps of émigrés, was also incorporated into Montalembert's corps. But, in spite of drafts from Europe, the legion was depleted by fever and casualties to 600 men. According to Montalembert, 'hardly a single day passed without our engaging the enemy and the corps being always either dispersed in the advanced posts, or placed at the head of attacking columns' (Simcoe

Papers). The corps was finally discontinued as of 25 June 1797. The remnants formed an independent troop of dragoons. The black auxiliary companies being incorporated into Dessource's, and the white companies became *Grenadiers britanniques de Saint-Domingue* until the evacuation from Haiti in October 1798. The uniform consisted of a round hat, a red coatee with red collar, yellow half-lapels, plain black cuffs with two small buttons under, white turnbacks, white metal buttons, white waistcoat and pantaloons, white accoutrements. The officers had the same uniform with silver epaulettes and buttons, a crimson sash and a small black plume on the round hat. The cavalry continued to wear the uniform of Charmilly's *Ulhans*. The artillery uniform is unknown.

Ulhans britanniques de Saint-Domingue (Charmilly's)

Authorised raised in British regular service On 9 December 1794, it was to consist of ten companies totalling 650 officers and men to be raised in Europe for service in Haiti under the command of Pierre-François Venault de Charmilly, formerly lieutenant-colonel of the *Légion de la Grande Anse*. About 360 men were raised, mostly ex-French prisoners of war, and sent to Haiti during 1795 to join about 75 cavalrymen from the *Légion de la Grande Anse* incorporated into the *Ulhans*. The corps was still 200 men short and was ordered incorporated to Montalembert's *Légion britannique de Saint-Domingue* on 8 December 1795. The uniform consisted of the British 'Tarleton' light dragoon helmet of black leather with black bearskin crest, red turban, black cockade and white plume; red coatee with red collar, yellow lapels with seven buttons each, black cuffs, blue turnbacks, white metal buttons; blue waistcoat and breeches and also linen pantaloons; light dragoon boots; cavalry cape; white accoutrements; and light cavalry saddlery. The *Ulhans* were armed with the light cavalry sabre, a pair pistols and a carbine but had no lances.

BLACK CHASSEURS

The terrible losses to the British army due to malaria and yellow fever drove the authorities to seek almost desperate solutions to find men to fight Toussaint L'Ouverture's French republican armies of freed blacks. The obvious answer was to raise units of armed black slaves to act as rangers, called *Chasseurs* in Saint-Domingue. The good performance of black corps, such as Kina's and Dessources, led General Williamson to order a general levy of *Chasseurs* corps on 26 June 1795.

The order decreed that one of every fifteen plantation slaves be drafted to form *Chasseurs* corps in the various parishes, the owners being compensated by government at the generous rate of £2,000 per man. These slaves would gain their freedom after five years of service. While they served, they were paid and fed as British soldiers and were allowed prize money as white troops. In spite of all this, the black soldiers were more economical than white soldiers since they did not have to be transported from Europe and were much less prone to sickness and desertion. It was considered especially urgent to raise Chasseurs corps at La Grande Anse and, on 3 July, the *Chasseurs de la Cayemitte* and the *Chasseurs des Irois* were ordered raised at once. Each was to have 528 blacks in 12 companies, commanded by white officers. On 28 December 1795, regulations specified the organisation of all *Chasseurs* corps to be of ten companies having each six officers, 56 other ranks including two sappers, two drummer and a fifer. Existing cavalry companies were to be abolished as the *Chasseurs* were to be only

Private of the 5th (Rifle) Battalion, 60th Foot, authorised in December 1797 and formed with Hompesch's and Lowenstein's Chasseurs in the West Indies. The uniform adopted was a black shako with green plume and cord around the top and white metal bugle badge, green coatee with red collar, cuffs, turnbacks and piping, green and red wings, pewter buttons, dark sky-blue trousers piped red, black short gaiters with red piping at top, black accoutrements. (Plate by P.W. Reynolds after a sketch by C.H. Smith)

infantry. From 25 June 1797, each company had an establishment of five officers, 87 other ranks including two drummers and a fifer, but excluding sappers. From mid-1795, the number of *Chasseurs* shot up from about 1,000 to over 4,300 by December 1795, 6,700 a year later and about

6,000 in June 1798. They formed the bulk of the colonial troops in British Haiti, were deployed in the countryside and did most of the fighting.

Their early uniforms appear to have been either green or red jackets with trousers and round hats. In July 1795, the *Chasseurs des Irois* and the *Chasseurs de la Cayemitte* were assigned 'a green jacket'. From early 1796, there was a basic uniform, common to all black *Chasseurs* units in Haiti, which would have included Kina's and Dessource's corps. This consisted of a round hat with a cockade and plume, a red jacket with collar and cuffs of a facing colour chosen by the colonel, a shirt and coarse trousers. Sappers in *Chasseurs* regiments had a 'red uniform jacket, a bearskin grenadier cap and a wide apron of white leather coming down to the knees' (T81/14). A waistcoat, a black stock, an extra shirt and an extra pair of Russia sheeting pantaloons were added in June 1797. Shoes were not generally worn by 'the beautiful black regiments...who, bare to the knee, made their way over ground' that booted Europeans would hesitate to tread, recalled a British military surgeon. They were armed with muskets and bayonets, had the usual accoutrements and machetes carried on a waistbelt.

BLACK REGULAR TROOPS

Two British sentries in Nassau, Bahamas, probably grenadiers belonging to the 47th Foot, c1798. They wear a uniform adapted for the West Indies: black round hats with white plume, red short-tailed coatee with white collar, cuffs and turnbacks – there is no lace except on the wings, white metal buttons, white gaiter-trousers. Detail is taken from a contemporary print. (Anne S.K. Brown Military Collection, Brown University)

Until the 1790s, West Indian garrisons were provided by British line regiments. The only colonial unit was the 300-strong 'Carolina Corps' serving in the Leeward Islands, said to have been formed from American loyalist blacks. The advent of war brought profound changes and many regular units composed of blacks were now raised.

Pioneers
On 16 October 1793, a Corps of Black Pioneers 'for the service in the West Indies' was authorised raised under the command of Lieutenant Colonel James Chalmers. This unit seems to have evolved into the 'Corps of Black Military Artificers and Pioneers'. In 1807, its establishment featured a cadre of ten sergeants, 18 corporals and two drummers drawn from British regiments and 300 black pioneers and 100 black artificers recruited from criminals 'guilty of the worst crimes' and black soldiers sentenced to death and 'pardoned [for] life'. Although under the 'Quarter & Barracks Department', the British cadres had 'the pay and allowances' of the Corps of Royal Military Artificers (CO 318/33).

Rangers
The harsh realities of West Indian warfare on British troops soon dictated the use of blacks as fighting soldiers in the Leeward and Windward islands. French royalist officers led the way in

'16th or Buckinghamshire Regt of Foot, undress worn on the expedition against Surinam in 1804.' They wore a black round hat with black cockade in front and a scarlet single-breasted coatee with yellow collar and cuffs, silver buttons, no lace, white turnbacks. Note the scarlet shoulder straps edged with silver lace instead of epaulettes. Gold gorget, crimson sash, white breeches, black boots and tassels. White shoulder sword-belt with silver oval belt-plate, gilt-hilted sword with black and gilt scabbard, sky blue water canteen with brown leather sling, white duck haversack, marked '16 Regt'. (Watercolour by C.C.P. Lawson after William Loftie. Anne S.K. Brown Military Collection, Brown University)

raising such units for the British. In 1794, Druault's Guadeloupe Rangers were raised in that island while Gaudin de Soter's Royal Island Rangers were forming in Martinique. British officers soon followed suit. In 1795, Captain Robert Malcolm raised his Royal Rangers in Martinique. Lieutenant Colonel James Seton organised the St. Vincent Rangers. In Grenada, there were the Loyal Black Rangers. Daniel O'Meara's 'Black Corps' was at St. Lucia, where it was joined by Druault's Guadeloupe Rangers in 1796. Both units saw much action on that island. A corps of 'South American Rangers' was also raised at Demerara in 1796. Druault's was sent to Trinidad in 1797 where it recruited anew and became the Trinidad Rangers. The Tobago Rangers participated in the failed attempt on San Juan, Puerto Rico, in 1797.

These black units, each usually about 200 or 300 men, proved to be very good. Sir John Moore wrote: 'In this country much may be made of black corps...they possess, I think, many excellent qualities as soldiers, and may with proper attention become equal to anything. Even as they are at present, they are for the West Indies invaluable.'

The Grenada Loyal Black Rangers wore round hats, red jackets with yellow collars and cuffs, shirts and blue trousers, a dress that must have been, with some variations, fairly common to most early black corps. Some, however, may have been dressed in white linen like the Demerara South American Rangers. Shoes do not seem to have been worn, at least not in the field.

Garrison Infantry

At St. Kitt's, by an act of 18 April 1795, some 500 slaves were selected to assist in the defence of the island, a number doubled over the next two years. Commanded by planters and drilled every Saturday, they would mobilise in the event of an attack. Sir John Moore felt this was 'a bad mode' and that blacks should be enlisted as regulars gaining their freedom at the end of their service. Forty of these slaves did serve full-time with the British garrison at the Brimstone Hill fortress, armed with pikes and cutlasses. Their uniform was a jacket, apparently white, faced with 'Red Cape [collar], Cuffs and Lapells, two Shirts and two pair of long Trousers with a Black Hat and Cockade and with a Belt for a Cutlass' (CO 240/14). In Dominica, the 250-strong Loyal Dominica Regiment was 'embodied, armed and disciplined' in December 1795 by drafting 2 per cent of the island's slaves (WO 1/82). They were 'to be armed and cloathed as soldiers' (CO 73/10). The uniform is unknown but the officers had gilt buttons marked with GR and the regi-

Painting said to represent Lieutenant Colonel Boyd Manningham with two black soldiers, c1796. The officer at centre-left wears a scarlet jacket with yellow cuffs and collar, silver buttons and lace, crimson sash, blue pantaloons, and a round hat with bearskin crest and white over red plume. The black soldier on the right is holding a pike and carrying a sword is a sergeant dressed in red with yellow collar and cuffs, white lace, white metal buttons, red sash, blue pantaloons with narrow red stripe, round hat with bearskin crest and white over red plume. The black soldier in the middle towards the back wears a black cap with a white metal star plate, blue jacket with red pointed cuff and collar, white metal buttons, white or buff gaiter-trousers, white accoutrements with brass oval belt-plate. (Manningham perished in Haiti. Rifle Brigade Museum. W.Y. Carman photo)

ment's name. Weapons consisted of muskets with bayonets and many probably carried machetes.

West India Regiments

The military authorities soon recognised the need for entirely black regiments in the British army. Despite much opposition from the various island legislatures, commissions were issued to colonels 1795 to raise eight such regiments, each to be commanded by white officers and NCOs. Each regiment was also to have a troop of light dragoons but, although officers were commissioned, few, if any, were actually raised. The first two regiments, Whyte's (numbered 1st in 1798) and Myer's (2nd), were commissioned on 24 April, followed by Keppel's (3rd), Nicolls (4th) and Howe's (5th) on 20 May, Whitelocke's (6th) on 1 September, Lewe's (7th) and Skerrett's on 15 September. Recruiting for these first eight regiments was slow, in 1796 Skerrett's was disbanded. The Carolina Corps and Malcolm's Royal Rangers were ordered incorporated into Whyte's and the St. Vincent Rangers into Myer's. Several regiments were also to be raised in Saint-Domingue but very few Haitians were actually enlisted. Colonial authorities feared that some of those recruits would spread revolutionary ideas to the British islands. Only cadres of Keppel's and Howe's were shuffled back and forth between Jamaica and Haiti between 1795 and 1797. It seems only Lewe's served permanently in Haiti, at Môle Saint-Nicolas, during 1796 and 1797.

The purchase of West African slaves was used to fill the ranks along with the incorporation of additional black corps. In 1798, five more regiments were commissioned. The 8th West India Regiment was authorised on 25 June by incorporating Cochrane-Johnstone's Loyal Dominica Regiment in August, the 9th incorporated the Trinidad Rangers, the 10th Soter's Island Rangers, the 11th the South American Rangers and the 12th O'Meara's Rangers. Reductions came following peace in 1802. The 8th was disbanded, the 9th, 10th and 12th were drafted into the 7th, the 11th into a new 8th. From 1804, the regiments had ten companies each, including flank companies. Eight West India regiments existed until 1816 when the 7th and 8th were disbanded, the 5th and 6th being reduced the following year and the 3rd and 4th in 1819.

A great fear of both the planters and the military authorities was that black soldiers would turn their weapons against their European officers and revolt. But such incidents proved rare. When they occurred they were due to gross mismanagement or misunderstanding by the officers. The worst case was the mutiny of the 8th West India Regiment in

Centre of the colours of the 4th West India Regiment, c1798 – yellow field, red oval at centre surrounded by a blue garter. Soldiers wore red coats faced yellow with round hats with fur crest, white waistcoat and breeches, white accoutrements. (National Army Museum, London, 1321)

Dominica during 1802. Colonel, Andrew Cochrane-Johnstone, was a corrupt rogue and tyrant who used his black soldiers as slaves to build up his estate, misappropriated funds and even kept a harem of black girls. In April, with arrears in pay of up to six months and ignorant of any other form of protest, part of the regiment mutinied at Fort Shirley murdering some of its officers. The revolt was bloodily put down by the 1st and 68th regiments, Royal Marines, seamen and Dominica militiamen. The 8th was disbanded but subsequent inquiries revealed Cochrane-Johnstone's exploitation and confirmed that, if treated fairly, the black troops were less prone to desertion and drink than Europeans and made excellent soldiers.

UNIFORMS OF THE WEST INDIA REGIMENTS

Little is known about the first uniforms of the West India regiments. The only solid indications are from figures of black soldiers shown on the remnants of the colours of the 4th West India Regiment. They are shown wearing black round hats with the brim edged with white lace, a black crest over the crown and a white plume; red coatee with yellow collar, cuffs and long lapels, white turnbacks, yellow epaulettes with fringes or tufts; tight white pantaloons tucked into black half-gaiters; white cross-belts with a brass oval belt-plate. This was likely typical of the uniforms worn from 1795 to about 1800 but the accoutrements may have been black in some of the other regiments. The 5th and 6th, however, were issued with white Russia Duck frocks and trousers, possibly round hats and woollen caps at that period and the 11th was also initially dressed in white.

The compilation known as the *1802 Clothing Regulations*, probably drafted between 1799 and 1802, gives the first extensive details on the uniforms of the 12 West India regiments. This called for a red jacket with red collar, the shoulder straps, small 'half' lapels and pointed cuffs of the facing colour, very short skirts which sloped off behind with no turnbacks. The half lapels each had three buttons and laced buttonholes, with eight small buttons below, two buttons under each cuff, one button and laced buttonhole on each side of the collar. Regimental lace edged the collar all around, the shoulder straps and the top of the cuffs and was used for the buttonholes of the half lapels and collar. Small white metal buttons were used. Sergeants had the same jacket but in scarlet cloth with white silk lace. The accoutrements were black.

The half lapels were initially fairly square, three inches wide at the bottom and four inches at the top, but Smith's drawing of a soldier of the 1st in c1808, and his plate of the 5th in 1814, shows them having become more rounded and pointing lower down. There were fewer buttons below the lapels. He also shows the line infantry's straight cuffs with buttons and buttonhole lace, and no lace or button on the collar.

Drummers had the same type of jacket but in the facing colour with red half lapels, cuffs, shoulder straps and wings. The lace was set as before and, in addition, at the seams and the wings. The drummer's lace was 'white and in the option of the Colonel' according to the 1802 Regulations.

Soldiers of the West India regiments were not issued with waistcoats but with two pairs of white duck gaiter-trousers yearly. On 7 July 1810, this was ordered changed to blue serge gaiter-trousers. Round hats were worn until 1803 and shakos issued every second year after that. These were the stovepipe shako and the 'Belgic' shako issued from 1812-1813.

The black accoutrements were ordered changed to white on 17 October 1803 but it took many years, perhaps until as late as 1812, before this change was completed. Undress consisted of white round jackets with collar and cuffs of the facing colour, loose white trousers and probably a fatigue cap. Shoes were issued yearly but the men were often more comfortable in bare feet.

Officers were to have, according to the 1802 Regulations, a scarlet coat with a scarlet collar, 'half' lapels and cuffs of the facing colour, the rest trimmed as the coats of line infantry officers, including long tails and white turnbacks. This was apparently not always closely followed after 1803 and while officers of the 4th, 5th, 6th and 8th are known to have had scarlet collars, those of the 2nd had collars of the facing colour with the coats

Private soldier of a West India regiment, 1803, second from left, possibly the earliest printed representation of these troops. From De Bosset's uniform chart. (Anne S.K. Brown Military Collection, Brown University)

being cut in similar fashion to those of line infantry officers. All wore white waistcoats and breeches or pantaloons, boots, bicorn hats and also wore round hats in undress.

The distinctions of the West India regiments were as follows:

1st: white facings; men's lace white with a black line; officer's lace silver.

2nd: yellow facings; men's lace white with a green, yellow and purple line (1802), a black and a yellow line (1814); officer's lace gold.

3rd: yellow facings; men's lace white with a wide black line; officer's lace silver.

4th: yellow facings; men's lace white with a blue line between two yellow lines; officer's lace silver.

5th: green facings, men's lace plain white; officer's lace gold.

6th: yellow facings; men's lace white with a black line; officer's lace silver.

7th: yellow facings; men's lace white with a brown, yellow and scarlet line (1802), with a black and yellow line (1814); officer's lace silver.

8th (1798-1802): grey or French grey facings; men's lace white with a red, yellow and black line; officer's lace unknown but probably gold as in the Loyal Dominica Regiment.

8th (1803-1816): green facings; men's lace plain white; officer's lace gold.

9th (1798-1802): yellow facings; men's lace white with two blue and a yellow line; officer's lace unknown.

10th (1798-1802): buff facings; men's lace white with a scarlet and black edge; officer's lace unknown.

11th (1798-1802): green facings; men's lace white with a narrow green edge; officer's lace unknown.

12th (1798-1802): buff facings; men's lace white with a scarlet and black edge; officer's lace unknown.

The men's lace is indicated as set evenly with square ends for all regiments but Pearse's tailoring notes of c1810 mention pointed lace for the men and drummers of the 3rd West India Regiment.

Surinam Chasseurs

A corps of *Neger Vrikops* or *Jägers* (black chasseurs or rangers) of 300 free blacks was raised by the Dutch in 1772 to serve against maroons in the interior of the colony and seems to have been kept in service during the first British occupation (1799-1802). After Surinam's recapture in May 1804, the black corps was incorporated into the new Surinam Chasseurs and formed three of its five companies. Each company had 110 men including five white sergeants and a bugler led by four European officers. A mutiny of a 20-man detachment at the outpost of Oranjebo occurred on 7 September 1805, spread to several other outposts resulting in about 80 black chasseurs joining the maroons. The subsequent inquiry arrived at the conclusion that the mutiny had been caused by maroons enlisted into the corps. The black *Jägers* were nicknamed *redimusu*, for the red caps they wore and do not seem to have had a proper uniform until they were reorganised by the Dutch as the 'Colonial Guides' in 1818.

Martinique Brigades

Two small ranger corps called 'brigades' of five to eight free black men each were organised in 1810 to chase maroons in the interior of Martinique. Each was armed with a musket and a sabre and wore a blue jacket, a shirt, linen trousers and shoes.

Black Garrison Companies

1st company formed at Jamaica on 1 August 1813, from black soldiers of the 2nd, 5th and 7th West India regiments who were unfit for active service but equal to garrison duty. It was disbanded in Trinidad on 24 August 1817. 2nd company formed at Curaçao on 25 June 1815, from the 5th and 7th West India regiment with European officers and NCOs from the disbanded 2nd European company and transferred to Jamaica in March 1816, disbanded on 24 July 1817.[1] Uniforms as the line infantry: shako, red coatee with white col-

Surgeon's coat of the 4th West India Regiment, c1803-1812. It is scarlet with yellow collar and cuffs, white turnbacks, silver buttons, twist cord at buttonholes. Surgeons did not have lapels. (Glenbow Museum Collection, Calgary, Alberta)

[1] As per A.S. White, 'Garrison, Reserve and Veteran Battalions and Companies', *Journal of the Society for Army Historical Research*, 1960, except for disbandment dates and locations given here according to The Military Register, 14 January 1818, p.67. White says the two companies were on 24 July 1817 in Jamaica.

Sketch of the officer's silver belt-plate of the 4th West India Regiment, c1796-1815. (Army Museums Ogilby Trust, London)

panies, totalling 199 officers and men, were sent to Haiti in April 1796, and posted to the Môle and Port au Prince. But they were reduced by yellow fever to just 39 by August 1797. Reinforced by recruits, detachments were involved in various skirmishes and in the recapture of Mirebalais and Grand Bois. They were evacuated to Jamaica in September 1798 where a third company joined the unit in December 1799. The corps was posted to Port Royal with a detachment in the Bahamas. Fevers continued to shrink its strength and the remnants were eventually amalgamated into the Royal Foreign Artillery in 1803. In 1796, the uniform included a blue jacket, probably faced red, a blue waistcoat, blue pantaloons, a grey round hat

lar, cuffs, shoulder straps and turnbacks; plain white lace, square ended and set evenly; white metal buttons. Officers had silver lace.

Dominica Rangers

The corps was formed in early 1814 by drafting free blacks to chase runaway slaves and maroons who were making the island of Dominica 'very far from tranquil'. By March 1814, they had destroyed many maroon camps in the woods but the problem was never quite settled and the Dominica Rangers existed until the abolition of slavery.

EUROPEAN COLONIAL TROOPS

Dutch Emigrant Artillery (Nacquard's)

This unit was formed in England during 1795 with refugee Dutch artillerymen under the command of Major F.A.F. de Nacquard. Its two com-

Ensign P. Innes, 8th West India Regiment, 1808. He wears a a black round hat with white over red plume and a scarlet coat with scarlet collar and green lapels, white piping, gold epaulettes and buttons, crimson sash, white shoulder-belt with gilt plate. Silhouette by Buncombe. (National Army Museum, London, 12564)

with black feather and cockade, a greatcoat, gaiters and a stock. Bombardiers had yellow epaulettes, corporals had a loop on their hats, sergeants had a gold band and loop, officers had a red and gold cord on their hats. All carried swords with red and orange sword knots. They also had white duck forage caps, jackets and sleeveless waistcoats.

Dutch colonial troops in British service

The Loyal Orange Battalion (Van Well's) was formed in April 1796, shortly after the surrender of Demerara, with Dutch colonial soldiers taken into British pay and formed into a four-company battalion which then formed part of the British garrison of Demerara and Berbice. They continued to wear the Dutch uniform consisting of a single-breasted blue short jacket with scarlet cuffs and collar. The 22-man artillery detachment had blue slop jackets.

The garrison of Surinam was also taken into British pay in September 1799, and formed into a Royal Dutch Battalion (Coehorn's) and two companies of Royal Dutch Artillery. A portrait of Colonel de Coehorn shows him in scarlet faced blue with silver lace, the letters R.D. (Royal Dutch) at the centre of a garter star on the silver epaulettes. The Royal Dutch Artillery had the same uniform as the Royal Artillery except for round hats with white plumes in front according to Hamilton Smith's notes. The garrison of Curaçao was taken into British service as well from September 1800. These units remained in British service until December 1802 when the occupied colonies were returned to Holland.

Foreign Artillery, Independent Companies of

When sent to the West Indies, La Tour's *Royal-Étranger* regiment and Lowenstein's Fusiliers each had an artillery company. In February and April 1798 they were drafted into a new Foreign Artillery corps as independent companies and stationed in Martinique with detachments at Trinidad, Tobago and St. Lucia. In June 1802, the 2nd company was transferred to Grenada. The majority of the men were Dutch and German while the officers were French émigrés. These companies were used to form the Royal Foreign Artillery in 1803. The uniform was probably the

Private of the 5th West India Regiment. Aqua-tint by Charles Hamilton Smith published on 2 January 1814. The private wears a black shako with brass plate, white cords and white over red plume, red jacket with red collar, green half-lapels, cuffs and shoulder straps, white lace and pewter buttons, and blue serge gaiter-trousers. In the background, a soldier wearing the regimental red jacket but with white pantaloons and gaiters with another soldier in the undress white jacket with green collar and cuffs. (Anne S.K. Brown Military Collection, Brown University, Providence)

same as the uniform worn by the Royal Artillery.

Royal Foreign Artillery

The corps was formed during March 1803 by incorporating various independent artillery units in the West Indies. It was to consist of three companies, known by their captain's names, under the command of Major de Nacquard, formerly of the Dutch Emigrant Artillery. A fourth company was

Major Edward Carey Fleming, 2nd West India Regiment, 1815. He wears a scarlet coat with yellow collar, gold epaulettes and buttons. (National Army Museum, London, 10156)

York Light Infantry Volunteers

The regiment was formed in Barbados during the autumn of 1803 from the soldiers of the captured Dutch garrisons of Demerara, Essequebo and Berbice who volunteered into British service. Later on, French deserters from Spain were sent to the corps. Most officers were British. First called the 'Barbados Volunteer Emigrants', the unit's name was changed to York Light Infantry Volunteers in January 1804. It served in Barbados and Dominica, took part in the capture of Martinique and Guadeloupe in 1809 and 1810. Afterwards it was posted to Barbados and Antigua, then in 1814, sent to Jamaica. The uniform was based on that of the 95th Rifles: green jacket with black collar, cuffs and shoulder straps all edged with white lace, three rows of white metal buttons and green pantaloons. The regiment apparently had drummers rather than buglers as it required six drums in 1813. The officer's dolman was green with black collar and cuffs and trimmed with three rows of silver buttons. The cords and embroidery were probably black. The corps initially had the black stovepipe shako, most likely with a bugle badge, but wore the infantry 'Belgic'

added in April 1806, but stayed as a depot in Lymington, England. Each company was to have 144 men plus three staff giving a total of 579 officers and men, but the actual strength was usually between 400 and 500.

Most of the officers were French émigrés while the men were usually Dutchmen or Germans. Capt. Prevost company was posted at Trinidad with detachments at St. Lucia, Barbados, Grenada and St. Vincent. Capt. de Menard's was in Jamaica with a detachment in Honduras. Capt. de Vellicy's was at St. Vincent with a detachment at Grenada. Detachments participated in campaigns against the French islands. The corps returned from the West Indies to Lymington on 26 October 1816 and was disbanded there on 31 January 1817. The uniform was similar to that worn by the Royal Artillery.

An officer's belt-plate design for the 3rd West India Regiment, c1815. It is made from silver with gilt mountings. As the 3rd called itself the 'Prince of Wales' West India Regiment it used the prince's feather badge and motto on its appointments. (Army Museums Ogilby Trust, London)

1: Ulhans britanniques de Saint-Domingue (Charmilly's), trooper, 1795
2: Dillon's Regiment (Saint-Domingue), private, 1793-96
3: Chasseurs des Irois & Chasseurs de la Cayemitte (Saint-Domingue), 1795

1 2 3

A

1: Legion britannique de Saint-Domingue (Montalembert's), private, 1795-97
2: Chasseur pioneer (Saint-Domingue), 1796-97
3: Chasseur private (Saint-Domingue), 1796-98

B

1: Chasseur or Ranger officer, c.1795
2: Grenada Loyal Black Rangers, private, 1796
3: Dominica Militia, artillery officer, c.1795

C

1: Martinique Militia, artilleryman, 1794-1802
2: 20th (Jamaica) Light Dragoons, trooper, 1796-97
3: St. Kitts Corps of Embodied Slaves, 1795

D

1: West India regiments, officer, c.1801-1803
2: 8th West India Regiment, private, c.1801-02
3: 4th West India Regiment, private, c.1795-1798

E

1: St. Kitts Militia, infantry private, 1805-06
2: Dominica Militia, infantry officer, 1805
3: Barbados Militia, Light Company, 1805

F

1: 1st West India Regiment, private, c.1803-1810
2: Royal West India Rangers, bugler, c.1810
3: 5th & 8th West India Regiments, sergeant, c.1808-12

G

1: Black garrison companies, private, 1813-16
2: 2nd West India Regiment, drummer, 1814-16
3: Royal York Rangers, private, 1808-13

H

shako from December 1813. It is shown as white by Hamilton Smith, but was reported as brown 'according to the late regulation' by an inspecting officer (WO 27/118). The regiment had white accoutrements. In 1817, it was sent to England and disbanded at Harwich on 19 March.

European Garrison Companies

Formed with men from European colonial regiments in the West Indies that had become unfit for active service but who could carry out garrison duties. The 1st company was ordered formed on 25 December 1803, in Jamaica, transferred to Nassau, Bahamas, in March 1808, returned to Jamaica in April 1814 where it was disbanded on 24 June 1817. The 2nd company was ordered formed 25 December 1803, in Barbados, transferred to the Bahamas in June 1808 and sent to Jamaica in April 1814 to be disbanded. The men were drafted into the 1st company, officers and NCOs into the 2nd Black Garrison Company.[2] Uniforms were as for the line infantry: red coatee with blue collar, cuffs, shoulder straps and white turnbacks; white lace with a yellow line, square ended and set evenly; white metal buttons. Officers had silver lace.

Surinam Chasseurs

This five-company unit included two of Europeans, each company having four officers and 110 men including a bugler, apparently recruited from the former Dutch garrison after the capture of the colony by the British in 1804. The corps was commanded by a major assisted by seven staff officers (WO 1/150).

Royal West India Rangers

Authorised on 25 October 1806, it was to consist of eight companies of 100 men each, formed from elements of the Royal African Corps. It was sent to the West Indies the following year, serving at Antigua, Barbados and St. Kitt's. Augmented to ten companies in 1807, it was a quasi-penal battalion composed mainly of British convicts and the worst of the French prisoners volunteered from

Private of the Black Chasseurs of Surinam. Engraving by William Blake, the celebrated poet who earned his living as an engraver, after a drawing by Gabriel Stedman for his **Narrative of a Five Years' Expedition Against the Revolted Negroes of Surinam** *(London, 1796). Stedman noted that it was the custom for blacks of both sexes in Surinam to be naked from the waist up. The chasseurs often followed this fashion although they seem to have had short green jackets. They were also issued with a pair of breeches, a red cap and were armed with a musket and a machete. This appears to have been their dress during the first (1799-1802) and perhaps the second (1804-1816) British occupation of Surinam.*

the hulks. Desertion was high and the corps was a source of anxiety for the authorities. But it gave good service in the campaigns against the French islands. The uniform was based on that of the 60th Rifles: green jacket with red collar, cuffs and shoulder straps all edged with white lace with a blue line, three rows of white metal buttons and blue pantaloons. Buglers had the same uniform but their jackets had wings and were trimmed with 16 yards of white half-inch lace with a blue zigzag applied at the seams, edging the cuffs, collar, shoulder straps and set in zigzag 'in the middle of [the] wings and collar' according to Pearse's

---

[2] As per A.S. White. According to the Public Record Office's *Alphabetical Guide to certain War Office and other Military Records* (London, 1931), the European Garrison Companies were raised in Trinidad and the West Indies and disbanded in Barbados in 1817 and the Bahamas in 1818.

Gunners of the Royal Artillery, 1807. They wore a black shako with brass plate and white plume, blue coatee with red collar and cuffs, yellow lace and brass buttons. The Royal Foreign Artillery in the West Indies had a similar uniform. Print after Atkinson. (Anne S.K. Brown Military Collection, Brown University, Providence)

tailoring note. The privates' and buglers' jackets apparently only had 20 buttons, probably set in three rows of six buttons each with two for the shoulder straps. Hamilton Smith's chart shows a broad white lace edging but this is not indicated in the tailoring notes. The officer's dolman was green with scarlet collar and cuffs and trimmed with three rows of gilt buttons. The cords and embroidery were probably black. The corps had the stovepipe shako, with a stamped brass bugle badge bearing the letters R.W.I.R. The accoutrements were black, which was 'calculated to last any length of time in the [West Indian] climate' (WO 27/141). In 1819, the regiment left St. Kitt's for St. John, New Brunswick (Canada), and was disbanded there in late June.

Royal York Rangers

This regiment became a separate unit of six, later seven, companies of 100 men each from the Royal African Corps serving at Guernsey on 25 June 1808 and was sent to the West Indies.[3] It was composed of condemned men, mostly Irish and British with some foreigners, who volunteered to escape the gallows. In spite of its 'penal battalion' character, it won praise from General Beckwith for its excellent conduct in the campaign against Guadeloupe and appears to have been a thoroughly efficient unit. It was later posted at Grenada. The uniform was 'green faced with red' (WO 3/194), based on that of the 60th Rifles: green jacket with red collar, cuffs and shoulder straps all edged with white lace with a blue line, three rows of white metal buttons and blue pantaloons. Buglers had the same uniform but their jackets had wings and were trimmed with 16 yards of five-eighths of an inch wide lace with a complicated yellow and black centre with a red line on white at each side. This was 'all round [the] Jacket Seams, Cuffs, wings, Collar and Skirts' and set in zigzag 'in the middle of wings & collar' according to Pearse's notes. The privates' and buglers' jackets apparently only had 20 buttons. The officer's dolman was green with scarlet collar and cuffs and trimmed with three rows of gilt buttons. The cords and embroidery were probably black. The corps initially had the stovepipe shako, most likely with a bugle badge, but later wore the infantry 'Belgic' shako, probably from 1813, and perhaps of white felt. A surviving 'Belgic' shako badge has 'Royal York Rangers' on scrolls below the cypher. In 1819, the regiment was sent to Canada and disbanded at Halifax on 24 June.

York Chasseurs

Authorised on 5 November 1813, it was formed on the Isle of Wight, mostly from Irish deserters. The unit was put into shape by strict discipline and sent to Barbados and St. Vincent in 1814. By then, it was considered 'a most efficient regiment' with 'the most united and happy corps of officers I ever knew,' according to Captain Joseph Anderson. In 1815, the regiment formed part of the expedition to Guadeloupe after which it

---

[3] Not to be confused with the short-lived York Rangers authorised in July 1803, stationed at the Isle of Wight and incorporated into the Royal African Corps in March 1805. The Royal African Corps was re-titled Royal York Rangers on 24 August 1807 and divided into two distinct corps on 25 June 1808. The four companies serving in West Africa re-assumed the title Royal African Corps. The six companies at Guernsey sent to the West Indies retained the title royal York Rangers.

returned to St. Vincent. The uniform was as the 60th Rifles: green jacket with red collar, cuffs and shoulder straps, three rows of white metal buttons and green pantaloons. Officers had the green dolman with scarlet collar and cuffs and trimmed with three rows of silver buttons, silver cords and embroidery instead of black. In 1819, the York Chasseurs were sent from Jamaica to Canada and disbanded at Quebec on 24 August.

MILITIAS

The various island militias of the British West Indies generally included all white and free black able-bodied men. The wealthier white militiamen usually formed cavalry units or officered the foot troops. As a rule, free black units had white officers. The militiamen were expected to provide their own weapons, ammunition and uniforms, and train regularly, usually once a month. The local legislative assemblies often provided arms and equipment. In emergencies, some trusted slaves might also be armed with 'offensive weapons' such as pikes or hangers, but not with firearms. During the Napoleonic wars, detailed measures were passed, notably dress regulations applicable to all, a sign of increased militarisation of the population during this troubled period. West Indian militias were not only for protection against foreign raids and invasions. Everyone from the rich white planter to the modest free black feared slave uprisings above everything else. So these militias were also a type of armed constabulary and were often called up for guard duties, patrols and expeditions against the runaway slaves.

Antigua

From the end of the 17th century, the militia of the island of Antigua was governed by the most extensive regulations in the British West Indies. In the 1790s and early 1800s, it consisted of two regiments of infantry, an independent infantry company, a squadron of dragoons and a battalion of artillery.

On 18 April 1793, the uniforms were specified in a long order, outlined here: the men of the Red

Sergeant and private of the York Light Infantry Volunteers. Aqua-tint by Charles Hamilton Smith published on 1 December 1813. The sergeant on the left wears the white undress jacket with black collar, cuffs and shoulder straps, crimson sash, white pantaloons, black gaiters, white accoutrements, black knapsack with white belts, brass hilted hanger. The soldier on the right wears the regimental green coatee with black collar, cuffs and shoulder straps, white piping and white metal buttons, green pantaloons and black gaiters. White shako with green plume and cords and brass plate. White accoutrements with brass belt-plate. (Anne S.K. Brown Military Collection, Brown University, Providence)

Regiment had a scarlet coat without lapels and 'no cuffs' but a scarlet turn-down collar, skirts lined with brown linen, yellow metal buttons, three buttons at the sleeve opening, cross pockets with three buttons, white waistcoat and breeches, plain black hat with black cockade. Grenadiers and light infantry companies had a scarlet jacket with black velvet turn-down collar, cuffs (with four buttons each) and lapels, yellow metal buttons set in pairs, and 'Lord Howe's Trousers'. The men of the Blue Regiment had the same uniform as the Red Regiment except that the grenadiers and light infantry companies had blue collar, cuffs and lapels. The men of the Independent Company had the same uniform as the Red Regiment but the sergeants had green cuffs and collar. Officers had scarlet coats with collar, cuffs and lapels, cross pockets with four buttons, white linen lining, white waistcoat and breeches, black hat and cockade. The officers of the Red Regiment had black facings (collar, cuffs and lapels) and gilt buttons and epaulettes. Those of the Blue Regiment had blue facings with silver buttons and epaulettes and those of the Independent Company had green facings with gilt buttons marked 'A.I.C.'. The Squadron of Dragoons had a scarlet coat, without lapels, with blue standing collar and round cuffs, blue shoulder strap laced with gold braid on each shoulder, white linen lining, gilt buttons, one on the cuff and three on the lower sleeve, four to each pocket, white waistcoat and breeches, hussar boots with silver spurs, black hat with black cockade. Dragoon officers had gold laced buttonholes and epaulettes. The Battalion of Artillery wore a blue coat with scarlet collar, cuffs and skirts, yellow metal buttons, seven on the front 'set-on one, two and four' but none on the cuffs and collar, plain black hat with gilt button and loop, black cockade, Lord Howe's trousers. Artillery pioneers had jackets instead of coats and wore round hats. Officers had blue coats with scarlet collar, cuffs, lapels and skirts, gold laced buttonholes.

The very elaborate uniform regulations of 7 December 1805, from which we only can give the main features, brought up the Antigua Militia to the latest military fashion. The Red Regiment then had a red coatee, black collar and cuffs, white lace set in pairs, white turnbacks, white 'Lord Howe's' trousers, black shako with visor, brass plate with the King's Arms, red over white tuft. Officers had long-tailed coats with lapels, just like the regulars, trimmed with gold lace. The Blue Regiment had the same uniform but with blue facings, officers also having coats with lapels and silver lace. The Independent Company had the same but green facings, its officers having coats with lapels and gold lace. The Squadron of Dragoons had scarlet full dress and blue undress uniforms requiring a long description. The Battalion of Artillery had a blue coatee with scarlet collar and cuffs, gilt buttons with three guns, white turnbacks, white

trousers, 'Plain Black Hats, Black Cockades, and White Feathers in front'. Officers had long-tailed coats with lapels and gold lace.

Bahamas

A Militia Act passed on 16 September 1793 required compulsory enlistment into district militia companies except for volunteer companies. Soon, there was a five-hundred-men militia regiment with a Volunteer Artillery Company and a Troop of Light Dragoons in Nassau. Crooked Island had an artillery and an infantry company. Exuma and Long Island had an infantry company each. The infantrymen were armed 'with a proper Musket or Fusil and Bayonet, a Cartouch Box', or, 'in lieu of a bayonet, a Cutlass' and, from 1796, the cavalrymen were to have each a carbine, a pair of pistols, a broad sword with accoutrements and saddlery as well as boots and spurs and 'the uniform of the…Troop'. Fines were used to procure 'Feathers, Drums, fifes, Colours, Standards and Trumpets' (CO 25/8 and 9). The militia was called out in August 1797 when a planned slave uprising fomented by 'French Negroes' from Haiti was discovered. Following the declaration of war by the United States in 1812, Militia Acts were passed in January 1813 and December 1814, concentrating on readiness with weekly parades and drills up to twice a week. All militiamen were to be dressed in a uniform consisting of 'a jacket and overalls…a Hat and Shoes' whose colours were decided by the unit commanders (CO 25/15 and 16). The Turks and Caico Islands were then dependencies of the Bahamas.

Barbados

The once powerful militia of Barbados had, by the end of the 18th century, fallen into some neglect. The new Militia Act of 7 January 1795 maintained a troop of Life Guards of 60 troopers, raised over a century before, and established a regiment of infantry for each of the island's eleven parishes. In all, this made a force of about 3,300 including about 400 free blacks. Regiments bore their parish names (St. George's, St. Ann's, etc.) – except for the 'First or Royal Regiment of Militia' at St. Michael's parish, which included the capital

Brass shako badge of the Royal West India Rangers, c1810. (Drawing by Don Troiani from fragments at Nelson's Dockyard Museum, English Harbour, Antigua)

Bridgetown. Militiamen were to have 'a jacket of such colour as may be by the Colonel, regulated, a black hat, white pantaloons and shoes' with musket, bayonet and accoutrements, the more wealthy being obliged to supply a full suit of regimental clothing with accoutrements to the less affluent white inhabitants. Each regiment was equipped with two field guns (CO 30/16). On 21 December, 1795, 300 militiamen were put on duty for a month. In early 1805, the presence of a French fleet in the area brought more legislation, a corps of Sea Fencibles was also raised among merchant seamen by Captain Kempt of the Royal Navy. Some militiamen were detached to Dominica where they behaved well in action. Although not caring if militiamen were 'in red or in grey coats', the governor proposed a standard uniform in 1805 consisting of a round hat with white over red feather for battalion companies, white for grenadiers and green for light infantry, 'a red waist jacket' with blue collar, cuffs and piping which seems to have been worn by some units (CO 28/73). Militia law later having lapsed, volunteers were organised in April 1808 until a new law was passed. They had round hats with plumes as before and red coatees with blue lapels, collars and cuffs. From January 1809, free blacks were required to serve in companies of less than forty men. The Barbados Militia's uniform was officially ordered to be: 'A red Coatee with blue facings [lapels], Cape [collar] and Cuffs, Yellow Metal Buttons, a black Hat, Cockade and feather or Tuft, red at the Base and white above for Battalion Companies, White for the Grenadiers and green for the Light Infantry and white Pantaloons & black Shoes, a white Shirt, black stock and Armed and accoutred with a Complete Musket to carry an Once Ball, Bayonet and flint, Pricker and Brush, white Cross Belts and Cartouch Box to hold twenty four Cartridges' (CO 30/19). Officers had gold buttons and lace. The Life Guards were reported wearing red coats with much gold lace in the early 18th century and it seems likely that these wealthy gentlemen tried hard to emulate the dress of their London namesakes.[4]

Belize (British Honduras)

From the 17th century, English wood cutters from Jamaica and their slaves exploited the forests bordering the bay on Honduras. In spite of Spanish attempts to destroy them, small settlements slowly took root, the most notable being the town of Belize. The British government was not anxious to set up a full-fledged colony there, but appointed a superintendent reporting to the governor of Jamaica in the late 18th century. By 1797, a Spanish attack was feared so the 'baymen' and their slaves held regular drills. A most unusual feature in Honduras was the custom allowing slaves to have firearms and they were reported to be superb marksmen. The organisation of these 'militiamen' seems to have been rudimentary. They apparently used their own weapons and had no uniforms, but they participated in defeating the Spanish at St. George's Cay in September 1798.

Curaçao (British)

During the British occupation (1807-1816) of this Dutch colony, able-bodied men were ordered to enrol in the militia during 1810, but the measure was widely ignored. Three years later, an attempt to form three militia artillery companies also met with little response in spite of repeated orders, fines and threats. It seems that the settlers showed no greater inclination to fight for the English than for the Dutch.

4 By 1841 however, the Barbados Life Guards had adopted a light dragoon style uniform: Blue cloth shako with a black plume, blue coatee with 'scarlet front and facings'. *The Barbadian*, 2 January 1841.

Shako plate of the Royal York Rangers, c1812-1816. (Reconstitution from brass fragments by Don Troiani)

Demerara (British Guiana)

This Dutch colony was occupied by the British from 1796 to 1801 and from 1803. It remained British after the Napoleonic wars and was united with Essequibo and Berbice to form British Guyana in 1831. The Dutch seemed pleased to see the British arrive and, according to Pinkard's *Notes on the West Indies*, the 'Corps of Demerara Volunteers in scarlet uniform' was soon parading with the British troops in 1796-1797. After 1803, the Demerara militia is said to have adopted the dress of the 1st Foot (Royal Scots): red faced blue with gold buttons and lace for officers.

Dominica

The militia of the island of Dominica had a large proportion of planters and traders of French, Spanish and Italian origin as well as British families. It therefore included 'all descriptions of white men' and free coloured men from 18 to 50 years of age and was considered in 'a very respectable state' by the 1790s. All militiamen had to supply themselves with uniforms but arms and accoutrements were provided by the island's government. The uniform of the militia infantry was, according to T. Atwood's *History of the Island of Dominica*, 'scarlet coats, with facings [lapels and collar] and cuffs of black velvet; that of the [militia] artillery, blue turned up with scarlet' – no doubt the same as the Royal Artillery.

Grenada

The 1,200 men of Grenada's militia saw much active service during Fédon's rebellion. According to the militia act of 1 July 1801, the militia had five regiments of infantry, two companies of artillery and a troop of light dragoons on the island of Grenada, and one infantry regiment on the dependent island of Carriacou. The dress of the militia, previously left to unit commanders, was then ordered to be, for infantry officers, a scarlet coatee with black velvet collar, cuffs and lapels, white turnbacks, 'narrow Silver Lace on the Button-holes, white metal Buttons, Silver Epaulets, crimson silk Sashes, white Vests, black Stocks, white Pantaloons, Half Boots, black round Hats, with black cockades, and red and white Feathers'. Infantry NCOs and privates were to have 'the same uniform...except for the Epaulets, Sashes and Lace'. The artillery officers had a blue coatee with red collar, cuffs and lapels, white turnbacks, gilt buttons, narrow gold lace at the button-holes, gold epaulets on the right shoulder, crimson silk sash, the rest being the same as the infantry except for a black plume on the round hat. The artillery privates had the same uniform but with no lace, epaulets or sashes. The light dragoon uniform is not mentioned.

Guadeloupe (British)

The island, except for a few months in 1794, remained French until captured by the British in 1810. The Guadeloupe militia was re-established by the British administration to insure interior security on 13 October 1810 but only the dragoons were allowed a pair of pistols and a sabre, the governor feeling it might be imprudent to permit arms to the others. Finally, on 10 June 1811, the militia was ordered reorganised by the British and the militiamen ordered to wear red coats and black cockades on their hats. This was not at all accepted by the proud Guadeloupeans. Neither fines nor threats made them register in the militia and wear the abhorred red coats: only a few civil servants and some English residents wore it.

Thanks to this 'public relations disaster' by the British, the Guadeloupe militia was all but nonexistent between 1811 and 1814.

Haiti (British)

Part of western and southern Haiti was occupied by the British from 1793 to 1798, a regime welcomed and supported by many creoles in the former French colony. The militia rallied to the royalist cause in British occupied areas and numbered about 3-4,000 men. Some were embodied and occasionally saw action. In June 1797, there were four embodied companies including 30 mounted men in Port au Prince. Croix des Bousquets had a company of cavalry and two of infantry, St. Marc's four infantry companies and Môle Saint-Nicolas 120 militiamen. The 'ancient ordinances for the Militia' being 'acceptable to the Inhabitants' the British kept these generally in force and this may have included uniforms.[5]

Jamaica

There were three regiments of cavalry, one for each county. The infantry amounted to 14 regiments in 1793 and 18 regiments ten years later. There were also a few artillery companies and, eventually, rifle companies. It represented a force of about 8,000 men of which some 3,000 were free blacks, the largest militia force in the British West Indies. All were to provide their own arms and equipment. Only from 1792 were the militiamen of Jamaica required to wear uniforms, the type and fashion being left to the commanders of units. This, when it was acted upon, must have produced some variety. Charles Hamilton Smith, who served on the island, noted that the three cavalry regiments had a light dragoon style blue jacket with yellow or buff collar and cuffs with white (silver for officers) cords and buttons.

Some Jamaican militia was deployed during the maroon uprising of 1795-1796 and mobilised again from February to October 1798 to deal with gangs of bandits in the Trelawny mountains. Special troops were needed to pursue them into the inte-

Light infantry company officer's coatee of the Barbados Militia, c1815-1820. It is scarlet with blue piped white collar, cuffs and lapels, white turnbacks, gold buttons and wings, and gold lace edging around the collar, top of the cuffs and lapels. (National Army Museum, London)

rior. Consequently, in June, the legislature embodied three companies of woodsmen composed of free blacks and Indians and also a body of loyal Accompong maroons, which soon dispersed the bandits.

The Militia Act of 9 December 1802 instituted standard uniforms for the various types of militias. NCOs and privates of infantry were to have 'a red coatee with blue facings [lapels], cuffs and cape [collar], and plain yellow buttons; white waistcoat, round black hat (except as to light infantry who may use caps [shakos]); black stock; white Russia sheeting or canvas pantaloons; and shoes. And the flank companies shall wear such feathers as the colonel or commanding officer of each regiment

5 Under the ordinance of 1 January 1787, the militia infantry had all-white uniforms with blue cuffs and lapels in the Western District, white cuffs and blue lapels in the South; the white dragoons had red coats with white lapels, cuffs, turnbacks, waistcoats and breeches; all the mulatto dragoons had nankeen surtouts with red cuffs and collars. All had white metal buttons.

Light cavalry officer's jacket of the Jamaica Militia. This garment, dark blue with buff collar and cuffs trimmed with silver cords and button, apparently dates from the 1820s but these colours and the light dragoon style were worn in many cavalry units since the 1790s in Jamaica. (National Army Museum, London, 23380)

shall order.' This was somewhat simplified by the Militia Act of 14 December 1809, which specified 'a scarlet jacket, with dark blue cuffs and cape [collar], and plain yellow metal buttons, white waistcoat, round black hat, black stock, white Russia sheeting or canvas pantaloons, and shoes'. It also called for 'every drummer, fifer, or musicians of every regiment' to have 'a dark blue jacket, with scarlet cuffs and cape [collar], plain yellow metal buttons' with hats and other garments as the rest of the men. The 1809 Act added dress instructions for rifle companies, which comprised 'a dark green cloth jacket and pantaloons, with yellow metal buttons, and green feathers'.

Militia artillery was prescribed, in the December 1802 Act, a uniform consisting of a 'dark blue coatee, with red facings [lapels], cuffs and cape [collar], with yellow buttons' and waistcoat, pantaloons, hats, stocks and shoes as the infantry. In 1809, this was altered to 'a dark blue jacket, with scarlet cuffs and cape [collar], plain yellow metal buttons'.

By the 1802 Act, the cavalry was to have 'a dark blue coatee with red facings [lapels], cuffs and cape [collar], and yellow buttons; white waistcoat; blue cloth or cassimere pantaloons; black stock; trooper's boots, with spurs; and a round black hat'. The 1809 Act called for a 'dark blue jacket, with white metal buttons, scarlet cuffs and cape [collar], blue cloth or cassimere pantaloons, black stock, trooper's boots with spurs, and a round black hat'. Not all troops adopted this dress, some keeping the silver braided blue faced buff light dragoon dress.

From 1802, Jamaican militia infantry and artillery officers were to wear a long-tailed coat with gold epaulettes and gorget, narrow gold vellum lace on the buttonholes of the coatees, white waistcoat and breeches, high black top boots, bicorn hat with cockade and feather, 'yellow mounted cut and thrust sword' with white shoulder sword-belt. The 1809 Act prescribed the men's short-tailed jacket to the officers, without vellum lace, worn with pantaloons and a round hat. Rifle officers had gold epaulettes. Cavalry officers had gold vellum lace and wings on the coatee from 1802 but this was changed to silver wings and no lace on the jacket from 1809, field officers having epaulettes. All had crimson sashes. The Cayman Islands were then dependencies of Jamaica and probably came under the same militia laws.

Martinique (British)

This important French island was occupied by the British from 1794 to 1802 and from 1809 to 1815. On 9 October 1794, a few months after the capture of Martinique, the British governor-general issued orders regarding the service of the militia in the various districts and prescribed the types of weapons and uniforms to be used. Militiamen of infantry companies were to be armed with a musket and bayonet and be equipped with a shoulder-belt holding a cartridge box and a waist-belt holding a belly box, both boxes containing a total of 60 rounds. The uniform was a red jacket with

Frenchmen and some 250 English militiamen, formed with newly arrived residents to the island. The militia remained the same until the island was returned to France in 1802.

Martinique fell again to the British forces in February 1809 and soon afterwards, on 23 March, the British authorities ordered that the militia continue to serve as previously for the 'police and interior security of the colony' and that the companies make an oath of allegiance. Time passed and by the autumn of 1811, it was felt that the militia should have a distinct 'colonial uniform' which was decreed on 30 September. The militia infantry was assigned a white jacket with red collar and cuffs, plain yellow buttons, white or nankeen waistcoat, pantaloons and gaiters, round hat and black cockade. Militia dragoons wore a green jacket with red collar and cuffs, two rows of buttons down the front, round hat and black cockade. The officers had 'the insignia of their rank' which apparently meant epaulettes.

Montserrat

This small and lush island was raided in March 1805 and July 1806 by French fleets. With no regular garrison, no major fortifications and a small militia, the inhabitants were reduced to paying the French to minimise the plunder in Plymouth, the island's only town. The Militia Act of 1777 mentioned white and free black companies wearing uniforms of their choice. Apparently, there was no new militia act until 1823. In 1811, there were about 250 militiamen of whom 154 were white and the rest free blacks. The practical uniforms specified in 1823 may well have been worn previously. It consisted of a black round hat with a cockade, a white Russia sheeting jacket with blue or yellow cuffs and collar, white waistcoat, trousers and gaiters, officers to wear the same with a crimson sash and a feather to the hat.

Saint Kitt's

The militia of St. Kitt's (also called St. Christopher's) consisted of the Windward Regiment and the Leeward Regiment along with a small troop of cavalry (disbanded in 1797). The infantry was armed with muskets and bayonets, cartridge boxes and white cross-belts, the

A 'captain' of the Jamaican Maroons in the uprising of 1795. Maroons were generally hardly dressed but were well armed. (Engraving after Bryan Edward's **Proceedings of the Government and Assembly of Jamaica in regard to the Maroon Negroes,** *London, 1796)*

pale yellow collar and cuffs, white metal buttons, grey waistcoat and pantaloons, round hat with a black cockade. Militia artillerymen had the same uniform except for black collar and cuffs to the red jacket. The militia dragoons wore a blue jacket with pale yellow collar and cuffs, white metal buttons, yellow nankeen waistcoat and breeches, boots, round hat and black cockade.

The dragoons were to be armed with a sword and pair of pistols, and equipped with a shoulder-belt for the sword, a belly box holding 20 rounds. The only distinction for officers was a gorget; they had no epaulettes. Sergeants had two diagonal white laces on the forearm of their jackets, corporals one. Thus reorganised, with due regard to 'proceed with great circumspection to avoid putting arms into improper hands' (WO 1/83), the Martinique militia soon had, by the spring of 1795, six battalions totalling about 2,200

Cuban Besucal Chasseur, 1796. A company of these men, specialised in hunting runaway slaves with their dogs, was hired by the legislature of Jamaica and deployed against the maroons in 1796. Each chasseur had three dogs trained to hunt blacks. Their dress consisted of a 'check shirt open at the collar, from which hangs a small crucifix; a wide pair of trowsers, also check; a straw hat...seven or eight inches in the rim, with a shallow round crown, and very light; add his belt and sword [actually a machete]...and a pair of untanned leather shoes. Into this dress put a man with a Spanish countenance, swarthy but animated, a person above the middle size, thin but not meagre; to his belt affix the cotton ropes, and imagine them attached by collars round the necks of his dogs...' (R.C. Dallas, History of the Maroons, London, 1803, Vol. 2)

cavalrymen with a pair of pistols and a 'cutting sword'. The Militia Act of June 1794 required rank and file militiamen to appear 'decently dressed in a blue Coat or Jacket with a white Undersuit'. Infantry officers appear to have worn scarlet uniforms faced blue with gold lace, and cavalry officers blue coats faced scarlet with gold lace.

From April 1795, the units' commanders could regulate their unit's uniforms. The following August, the uniforms were ordered to be the 'same quality' as those of the regulars and militiamen could also have 'white short Jackets with a Yellow Cape [collar] and Cuffs' (CO 240/14).

Saint Vincent

The militia St. Vincent and its dependencies, the small islands of Bequia, Canouan and The Union, was well organised and quite active during the Carib's uprising of 1795-1796. Details on the dress and equipment of the militia were, however, only announced in the Militia Act of 8 October 1806. The Troop of Horse had a blue jacket with 'brimstone-coloured cloth' collar and cuffs, 'trimmed with gold braid or gold lace for the officers and Prussian binding for the privates, yellow metal buttons...gilt scales on both shoulders of the jacket' with white waistcoat and pantaloons, black cravat, 'black hats or helmets with bearskin, black cockade with red feather, half boots with spurs, and a blue cloak to fix behind the saddle' and a crimson sash for officers. The two regiments and five independent companies of infantry were all ordered to have 'a short scarlet cloth coat with deep blue facings' light infantry style, with gold lace on the officers' coats, 'yellow metal buttons, plain round black hats with cockade and feather' and white waistcoat and trousers, black gaiters 'to reach the knees' with black half boots and crimson sash with 'one or two epaulettes according to rank' for officers. The artillery company was to wear the same uniform as the Royal Artillery.

Tobago

Following an aborted slave uprising, a two-battalion militia regiment was established in this captured French island on 22 March 1803, but to serve just 'for the Sole Purpose of Defence against Internal Insurrection [by slaves], and Repelling the Attacks of Marauders [maroons]'. In about 1809, another Militia Act was passed calling for a nine-company regiment, a troop of cavalry in the town of Scarborough, and an artillery company of five officers, 13 master gunners and the remainder composed of 'free people of colour'. The 1803 infantry uniform consisted of a scarlet coat with blue collar, cuffs and half lapels, white turnbacks, gold buttons with the island's arm in relief, a white waistcoat, a pair of 'long white trousers with nine buttons from the ankle upwards' and a 'plain round black hat' with a cockade and a black stock. Officers had gold vellum lace at the buttonholes, gold epaulette on the right shoulder, crimson sash, 'cut and thrust

Brass belt plate of the Jamaica Militia, 1803. The alligator was the island's badge. (Journal of the Society for Army Historical Research)

sword, handle double gilt' with a shoulder-belt, the belt-plate and the sword guard to have the arms of the island. The sergeant had a scarlet strap edged with gold lace on each shoulder, the corporal's edged with gold cord and the private's was plain. The 1803 Act also specified that 'upon actual service in the woods, the officers and privates shall appear in green jackets, or such other colour as may be most convenient or least glaring' – but this was not required in the later Act.

The c1809 Act specified a similar uniform for the infantry officers adding a white feather to the hat; changed the gaiter-trousers to white pantaloons and half boots; 'sergeants to have on their coats a scarlet strap to each shoulder edged with gold vellum, and be armed with a Sword and halberd; the coats of the corporals are to have scarlet straps and no epaulets, sword or sash, and the uniforms of the privates to have the same as that of the commissioned officers except the epaulet, sword and sash, and to be armed with a good musket and bayonet, cartouch box, and white belts'. The troop of cavalry had 'a helmet, with bearskin and yellow leather, blue coat, waistcoat

and pantaloons with silver lace, and the officers to have silver epaulets, a bay or black horse' for all with saddlery and 'a pair of pistols, cartouche box and sabre'. The artillery uniform was to be the same as the infantry but 'substituting blue instead of scarlet, and scarlet instead of blue' (CO 287/3).

Trinidad

The British governor of this island captured from the Spanish in 1797, Sir Thomas Picton, who later gained lasting fame with Wellington, soon reorganised the island's militia in response to invasion threats from Venezuela and Guadeloupe. The militia eventually featured, by 1814, three infantry regiments, a brigade of artillery, a regiment of light dragoons, a regiment of hussars, three corps of mounted chasseurs, eight independent district companies and two battalions of Sea Fencibles. The Royal Trinidad Infantry Regiment and the cavalry included only white men with other units being generally composed of free blacks with white officers. According to a list published later, but probably reflecting dress adopted before 1815, the officers of the Royal Trinidad and the Diego Martin regiments wore scarlet faced blue with gold lace, the Loyal Trinidad Regiment had scarlet faced green with gold lace, the Royal Trinidad

Brass cartridge box plate of the Jamaica Militia, c1803. (Journal of the Society for Army Historical Research)

43

Light Dragoons had blue faced buff with silver lace, the Mounted Chasseurs had green faced red with gold lace and the Royal Trinidad Artillery had blue faced red with gold lace. From about 1806, some militiamen, probably mostly belonging to the Royal Trinidad Regiment in Port-of-Spain, had scarlet coatees of sergeant's quality given to them along with old muskets and accoutrements. All of these were still in use eight years later.

Virgin Islands and Tortola

The Militia Act of 26 March 1793 specified a red coat 'with short skirts' and blue collar, cuffs and lapels, 'yellow buttons, a black Hat turned up on the left side with a black cockade and white Lord Howe' trousers. The Act of 4 June 1796 called for a similar dress but no longer mentioned the hat being turned up but added a black plume to it as well as a black stock (CO 315/2).

THE PLATES

A1: Ulhans britanniques de Saint-Domingue (Charmilly's), trooper, 1795

This corps, equipped as British light cavalry, was incorporated into Montalembert's Legion most likely keeping the same uniform. (Grouvel)

A2: Dillon's Regiment (Saint-Domingue), private, 1793-1796

This battalion of the French army joined the British forces in Haiti. It continued to wear the red uniform of the Irish regiments in the old French royal army. (Grouvel)

A3: Chasseurs des Irois and Chasseurs de la Cayemitte (Saint-Domingue), 1795

These battalion-sized units had green jackets, possibly with the fashionable three rows of buttons, and probably wore round hat or caps and pantaloons. (T81/14)

B1: Légion britannique de Saint-Domingue (Montalembert's), private, 1795-1797

This regular colonial unit, which was recruited from white creoles in Saint-Domingue and

Red coatee of the Jamaica Militia with blue collar, cuffs and shoulder straps, white turnbacks and brass buttons, c1810-1815. (National Army Museum, London, 12419)

French émigrés from Europe saw much action, . (Grouvel)

B2: Chasseur pioneer (Saint-Domingue), 1796-1797

Each chasseur company had two pioneers until mid-1797. Even in tropical Haiti, they had bearskin caps and white aprons. Their jackets probably had extra trimmings such as lace and wings. (T81/14)

B3: Chasseur private (Saint-Domingue), 1796-1798

Over 6,000 chasseurs served the British cause in Haiti and did most of the fighting in this practical dress. (T81/14)

C1: Chasseur or Ranger officer, c1795

The dress adopted by the white officers of the new black light infantry units – *Chasseurs* in Saint-Domingue or the Rangers in the Windward

Back view of a coatee of the Jamaica Militia, c1810-1815. Note the absence of pocket flaps. (National Army Museum, London, 12420)

and Leeward Islands – was usually just a more elaborate version of their unit's basic uniform. (Portrait of Coote Manningham, Rifle Brigade Museum)

C2: Grenada Loyal Black Rangers, private, 1796

This unit was raised in 1795 and it served with distinction in Grenada. Nearly all ranger corps were incorporated into the West India regiments but the Grenada Loyal Black Rangers remained an independent unit until it was disbanded in 1818. Its dress was typical of black ranger units in the British islands during the 1790s. (Alexander McCombie, *The Laws of Grenada and the Grenadines, from the year 1766*, Grenada, 1830)

C3: Dominica Militia, artillery officer, c.1795

West Indian militias often mixed British Army regulation styles with round hats and pantaloons, then very popular in the tropics. (Thomas Atwood, *History of the Island of Dominica*, London, 1791)

D1: Martinique Militia, artilleryman, 1794-1802

The militia artillery of this former French island was unusual since it featured a red coat rather than the gunner's usual blue uniform. (Durand-Molard, *Code de la Martinique*, St. Pierre, Martinique, 1811, Vol. 4)

D2: 20th (Jamaica) Light Dragoons, trooper, 1796-1797

This unit was raised in England during 1791 for service in Jamaica. The uniform was blue with yellow facings and silver lace for officers. The headdress was a tin Grecian-style cap, officially prescribed in January 1796 to all light dragoon regiments in the tropics. The regiment left Jamaica for England in 1802. (WO 3/28; R. Marrion and D. Hagger, 'Forgotten Regiments: the 20th Hussars', *Military Modelling*, October 1993)

D3: St. Kitt's Corps of Embodied Slaves, 1795

Hundreds of slaves were selected to be trained weekly and 40 served with the regulars at Brimstone Hill. They were uniformed but local planters obviously also feared a mutiny and they were armed only with edged weapons. (CO 240/14)

Although the Jamaican Militia Acts specified plain buttons, some militiamen had them stamped with the island's alligator badge. (National Army Museum, London, 12421)

Private of the Royal Marines, 1815. Sea-soldiers were involved in many West Indian battles during the Napoleonic wars. Three companies of Royal Marines were formed with American refugee blacks in 1814 and disbanded in Trinidad during 1815. Round hat with white trim and white over red plume, red coatee with blue cuffs, collar and shoulder straps, pewter buttons, white lace with red and blue lines, white turnbacks and breeches, black gaiters, white accoutrements with brass plate. Print after Charles Hamilton Smith. (Anne S.K. Brown Military Collection, Brown University, Providence)

E1: West India regiments, officer, c1801-1803

The officer's uniform of the West India regiments mentioned in the '1802 regulations' with its scarlet collar and somewhat shorter lapels was distinct from the line regiments. The yellow facings and silver buttons shown on this figure are known to have been worn by officers of the 3rd, 4th, 6th and 7th regiments.

E2: 8th West India Regiment, private, c1801-1802

At the turn of the 19th century, the standard dress of the West India Regiments was short-tailed jackets with half lapels, gaiter-trousers, round hats and black accoutrements. The hue of the 8th's grey facings is given as French grey by Charles Hamilton Smith. (Houghton Library, Harvard University)

E3: 4th West India Regiment, private, c1795-1798

This figure is based on the earliest known rendering of a West India Regiment soldier embroidered on the colours of the 4th. Note the long lapels, crested round hat and white accoutrements. (National Army Museum, London)

F1: St. Kitt's Militia, infantry private, 1805-1806

This militiaman wears his civilian clothes with the militia's temporary white jacket with yellow cuffs, collar and white accoutrements. This was probably the dress of many men hastily called up during the French raids of 1805 and 1806. (CO 240/14)

F2: Dominica Militia, infantry officer, 1805

Officers of West Indian militias generally adopted uniforms which closely followed that of the regulars except for round hats which usually remained the official headdress. This Militia helped repulse the French attack on Roseau in 1805.

F3: Barbados Militia, Light Company, 1805

The uniform shown is according to a proposal by the governor of Barbados, Lord Seaforth, and seems to have been already worn by the St. George's Regiment. About 100 militiamen from this unit helped defend Dominica in 1805. (CO 28/73; R. Canon, *History of the 46th Foot*)

G1: 1st West India Regiment, private, c1803-1810

Wearing the stovepipe shako authorised to West India regiments from 1803. White accoutrements were authorised the same year but the black ones, if serviceable, often remained in use for may years thereafter. (Watercolour by Charles Hamilton Smith, Houghton Library, Harvard University)

G2: Royal West India Rangers, bugler, c1810

This unit wore green faced red, the buglers coatees trimmed with white lace bearing a blue zig-zag. (Pearse Notebook, Canadian War Museum)

G3: 5th and 8th West India Regiments, sergeant, c1808-1812

Sergeants of West India regiments were initially British although black soldiers began to be promoted to NCOs as time passed. They were armed with swords and pikes and had the same rank badges as those worn in the line infantry.

H1: Black garrison companies, private, 1813-1816
Veteran soldiers of the West India regiments who were fit for garrison duty were posted to these two companies. Unlike the West India regiments, the coatee was similar to that worn in the line infantry. (C.H. Smith, *Costume of the Army...*)

H2: 2nd West India Regt, drummer, 1814-1816
Drummers of the West India regiments wore 'reversed' colours as in the rest of the Army, in this case yellow faced with red. During this period, 'Belgic' shakos and blue gaiter-trousers were worn. The devises on the drum are after those on the regimental buttons.

H3: Royal York Rangers, private, 1808-1813
The British colonial regiments in the Caribbean recruited from Europeans generally wore the green jacket, in this case faced with red and edged white. (Pearse Notebook, Canadian War Museum)

SELECT BIBLIOGRAPHY

Books and articles: C. T. Atkinson, 'Foreign Regiments in the British Army, 1793-1802', *Journal of the Society for Army Historical Research*, XXII, 1943/4.

Timothy Ashby, *Shoulder belt plates, and badges recovered from Fort George, Grenada, West Indies, December 1969 to September 1972,* unpublished paper.

O.N. Bolland, *Colonialism and Resistance in Belize* (Belize 1988).

Roger N. Buckley, *Slaves in Red Coats: the British West India Regiments, 1795-1815* (Yale 1979).

J.E. Caufield, *One Hundred Years History of the 2nd Battalion West India Regiment* (London 1899).

J.F. Maurice (ed), *Diary of Sir John Moore*, Vol. 1. (London 1904).

Narda Dobson, *A History of Belize* (London 1973).

Henry Dow, *The Militia and Volunteers in Trinidad* (1958 unpublished paper).

Michael Duffy, *Soldiers, Sugar, and Seapower* (Oxford 1987).

Alfred B. Ellis, *History of the First West India Regiment* (London 1885).

John W. Fortescue, *A History of the British Army*, Vols. IV, V, X. (London 1915-1921).

David Patrick Geggus, *Slavery, War, and Revolution: The British Occupation of Saint-Domingue, 1793-1798* (Oxford 1982).

Louis de Grouvel, *Les corps de troupes de l'émigration française (1789-1815)*, Vol. 1. (Paris 1957).

James, William, *The Naval History of Great Britain*, Vols. 2 and 3. (London 1902).

Charles W.E. Jane, *Shirley Heights: The Story of the Redcoats in Antigua, English Harbour* (Antigua 1982).

E.L. Joseph, *History of Trinidad* (Trinidad 1837).

Roger N. Buckley (ed), *The Haitian Journal of Lieutenant Howard, York Hussars, 1796-1798* (U. of Tennessee 1985).

Philip Haythornthwaite, *The Armies of Wellington* (London 1994).

Lennox Honeychurch, *The Cabrits and Prince Ruperts Bay* (Roseau, Dominica Institute 1982).

Wim Hoogbergen, *The Boni Maroon Wars in Suriname* (Leiden 1990).

Vincent K. Hubbard, *Swords, Ships and Sugar: A History of Nevis to 1900* (Charletown, Nevis 1993).

M.E.S. Laws, *Battery Records of the Royal Artillery* (Woolwich 1952) and 'Foreign Artillery Corps in the British Service', *Journal of the Royal Artillery* (1938, 1946, 1948).

Cecil C.P. Lawson, *A History of the Uniforms of the British Army*, Vols. 4 and 5. (London 1966-1967).

Robert M. Marrion, 'The West India Regiments', *Military Modelling* (June and July 1987).

Charles Hamilton Smith, *Costume of the Army of the British Empire* (London 1815).

Marion M. Wheeler, Montserrat, *West Indies: a chronological history* (Montserrat National Trust 1988).

Periodicals: Annual Register (1793-1815); Journal of the Barbados Museum and Historical Society; London Chronicle (1794-1798).

Manuscripts: Archives of Ontario, Simcoe Family Papers; Army Museums Ogilby Trust, West Indies files; Canadian War Museum, J.N. and B. Pearse notebook; Public Records Office documents from the following series: Colonial Office 25 (Bahamas), 28 and 30 (Barbados), 73 (Dominica), 240 (St. Christopher's), 255 (St. Lucia), 287 (Tobago), 315 (Virgin Islands and Tortola), 318 (West Indies, general); Treasury 81; War Office 1 (In-letters), 3 (Commander-in-Chief, Out-letters), 27 (Inspections).

Notes sur les planches en couleur

A Ulhans britanniques de Saint-Domingue (Charmilly), soldat de cavalerie, 1795, équipés comme la cavalerie légère britannique et incorporés dans la Légion de Montalembert. Régiment de Dillon (Saint-Domingue), simple soldat, 1793–1796. Chasseurs des Irois & Chasseurs de la Cayemitte (Saint-Domingue), 1795, unités de la taille d'un bataillon avec veste verte, sans doute ornée du triple rang de boutons à la mode et sans doute coiffés de chapeaux ronds ou de calots, avec un pantalon bouffant (T81/14)

B Simple soldat de la Légion britannique de Saint-Domingue (Montalembert), 1795-7, unité coloniale régulière, qui participa à de nombreux affrontements et dont les recrues provenaient des créoles blancs de Saint-Domingue et d'émigrés français en Europe. Chasseur sapeur (Saint-Domingue), 1796–7. Chaque compagnie de chasseurs avait deux sapeurs jusqu'à mi-1797. Même sous le climat tropical de Haïti, ils portaient un bonnet de poil et un tablier blanc. Chasseur (Saint-Domingue), 1796-8. Plus de 6000 chasseurs servirent la cause britannique à Haïti et participèrent à la plupart des combats dans cet uniforme pratique. (T81/14)

C Chasseur ou officier ranger, vers 1795. L'uniforme adopté par les officiers blancs des nouvelles unités d'infanterie légère noires était généralement une version plus sophistiquée de l'uniforme de base de leur unité. Pratiquement tous les corps de rangers' furent incorporés dans les régiments des Antilles mais les Grenada Loyal Black Rangers restèrent une unité indépendante jusqu'à leur dissolution en 1818. Leur uniforme était typique des unités de rangers noires dans les îles britanniques vers 1790. Dominica Militia, officier d'artillerie, vers 1795. Les milices antillaises mélangeaient souvent les styles officiels de l'armée britannique avec des calots ronds et des pantalons bouffants, qui étaient alors très prisés sous les tropiques.

D Martinique Militia, artilleur, 1794–1802. La milice d'artillerie de cette ancienne île française était inhabituelle car elle portait un manteau rouge au lieu de l'uniforme bleu habituel des artilleurs. 20th (Jamaica) Light Dragoons, soldat de cavalerie, 1796–1797. Cette unité fut recrutée en Angleterre en 1791 pour servir en Jamaïque. L'uniforme était bleu avec parements jaunes et galon argent pour les officiers. Le couvre-chef était un calot de style grec, officiellement exigé en janvier 1796 pour tous les régiments de dragons légers sous les tropiques. St. Kitt's Corps of Embodied Slaves, 1795.

E Régiments des Antilles, officier, vers 1801-1803. L'uniforme des officiers des régiments des Antilles avec son col écarlate et ses revers un peu plus courts, était différent de celui des régiments de ligne. On sait que les officiers des 3ème, 4ème, 6ème et 7ème régiments portaient les parements jaunes et les boutons argentés dépeints ici. 8th West India Regiment, simple soldat, 1801–1802. Au début du 19ème siècle, l'uniforme standard des régiments des Antilles était composé d'une veste àpans courts avec un demi-revers, de pantalons serrés au mollet, d'un chapeau rond et d'accoutrements noirs. 4th West India Regiment, simple soldat, vers 1795–1798. Notez les longs revers, le chapeau rond à cimier et les accoutrements blancs.

F St. Kitt's Militia, simple soldat d'infanterie, 1805–1806. Ce soldat de milice porte ses vêtements civils avec la veste blanche temporaire de la milice, aux poignets et col jaunes avec accoutrements blancs. C'était comme l'uniforme de nombreux hommes appelés en hâte durant les attaques françaises de 1805 et 1806. Dominica Militia, officier d'infanterie, 1805. Les officiers des milices antillaises adoptaient généralement des uniformes très proches de ceux des militaires de carrière, àl'exception du chapeau rond qui restait généralement le couvre-chef officiel. Barbados Militia, Light Company, 1805.

G 1st West India Regiment, simple soldat, vers 1803–1810, qui porte le shako tuyau de poêle que les régiments des Antilles furent autorisés à porter à partir de 1803. Les accoutrements blancs furent autorisés la même année mais les noirs, s'ils étaient en état, continuèrent d'être utilisés pendant de nombreuses années. Royal West India Rangers, clairon, vers 1810. Cette unité portait du vert au parements rouges, la veste àcourte basque des clairons était bordée d'un galon blanc orné d'un zig-zag bleu. 5th et 8th West India Regiments, sergent, vers 1808–1812.

H Compagnies de garnisons noires, simple soldat, 1813–6. Les anciens combattants des régiments antillais capables de prendre un poste de garnison étaient placés dans ces deux compagnies. La veste à courtes basques était similaire à celle portée dans l'infanterie de ligne. 2nd West India Regt, tambour, 1814–1816. Les tambours des régiments antillais portaient des couleurs 'inversées', comme dans le reste de l'armée. Ici, il s'agit de jaune aux parements rouges. Durant cette période, on portait un shako 'Belgic' et des pantalons bleus serrés au mollet. Les devises inscrites sur le tambour sont inspirées des boutons des régiments. Royal York Rangers, simple soldat, 1808–1813. Les régiments coloniaux britanniques aux Caraïbes recrutés parmi des européens portaient généralement une veste verte, dans ce cas avec des parements rouges et bordée de blanc.

Farbtafeln

A Ulhans britanniques de Saint-Domingue (Charmillys), einfacher Soldat, 1795, der mit Ausstattung für die britische leichte Kavallerie in die Legion von Montalembert einbezogen wurde. Dillons Regiment (Saint-Domingue), Gefreiter, 1793–1796. Chasseurs des Irois & Chasseurs de la Cayemitte (Saint-Domingue), 1795, Einheiten von der Größe eines Bataillons mit grünen Jacken, möglicherweise mit den modischen drei Reihen von Knöpfen, und wahrscheinlich Rundhüten beziehungsweise Mützen und langen Hosen. (T81/14)

B Gefreiter der Légion britannique de Saint-Domingue (Montalemberts), 1795–7, eine reguläre Kolonialeinheit, die oft in Gefechte verwickelt war. Sie wurde aus weißen Kreolen in Saint-Domingue und französischen Emigranten aus Europa zusammengestellt. Chasseur-Pionier (Saint-Domingue), 1796–7. Bis Mitte 1797 verfügte jede Chasseur-Kompanie über zwei Pioniere. Selbst im tropischen Klima von Haiti trugen sie Bärenfellmützen und einen weißen Schurz. Chasseur-Gefreiter (Saint-Domingue), 1796–8. In Haiti dienten über 6000 Chasseurs der britischen Sache und übernahmen in dieser praktischen Uniform den Großteil des Kampfgeschehens. (T81/14)

C Chasseur bzw. Ranger-Offizier, ca. 1795. Die Kleidung, die sich die weißen Offiziere der neuen schwarzen leichten Infanterie zu eigen machten, war normalerweise eine etwas aufwendigere Version der Grunduniform ihrer Einheit. Fast alle Ranger-Korps wurden in die Regimenter auf den Westindischen Inseln aufgenommen, aber die Grenada Loyal Black Rangers blieben eine unabhängige Einheit, bis sie 1818 aufgelöst wurde. Die Kleidung war typisch für die schwarzen Ranger-Einheiten auf den britischen Inseln um 1790. Dominica Militia, Artillerieoffizier, ca. 1795. Die westindischen Milizen mischten häufig die Kleiderordnung der britischen Armee mit Rundhüten und langen Hosen, die zur damaligen Zeit in den Tropen sehr populär waren.

D Martinique Militia, Artillerist, 1794–1802. Die Miliz-Artillerie dieser ehemals französischen Insel war dadurch ungewöhnlich, daß sie einen roten Rock anstelle der gängigen blauen Uniform der Schützen aufwies. 20th (Jamaica) Light Dragoons, einfacher Soldat, 1796–1797. Diese Einheit wurde im Verlauf des Jahres 1791 in England für den Dienst auf Jamaik zusammengestellt. Die Uniform war blau mit gelben Blenden und Silbertresse für Offiziere. Auf dem Kopf trug man eine Zinnkappe im griechischen Stil, die im Januar 1796 für alle leichten Dragoner-Regimenter in den Tropen zu Vorschrift wurde. Das St. Kitt's Corps of Embodied Slaves, 1795.

E Westindische Regimenter, Offizier, ca. 1801–03. Die Offiziersuniform de westindischen Regimenter mit ihrem scharlachroten Kragen und den etwas kürzeren Revers unterschied sich von der der Mannschaftsgrade. Es ist bekannt, daß die gelben Blenden und silbernen Knöpfe, wie sie an dieser Figur ersichtlich sind, von den Offizieren der 3., 4., 6. und 7. Regiments getragen wurden. 8th West India Regiment, Gefreiter, ca. 1801–1802. Zu Anfang des 19. Jahrhunderts bestand die Standarduniform der westindischen Regimenter aus kurzschößigen Jacken mit halbem Revers, Gamaschenhosen, Rundhüten und schwarzer Ausrüstung. 4th West India Regiment, Gefreiter, ca. 1795–1798. Man beachte die langen Revers, den Rundhut mit Emblem und die weiße Ausrüstung.

F St. Kitt's Militia, Infanteriegefreiter, 1805–1806. Dieser Milizionär trägt im Grunde seine Zivilkleidung mit der provisorischen weißen Milizjacke mit gelben Manschetten und Kragen und weißer Ausrüstung. So waren wahrscheinlich die meisten Männer gekleidet, die während der französischen Überfälle der Jahre 1805 und 1806 hastig einberufen wurden. Dominica Militia, Infanterieoffizier, 1805. Die Offiziere der westindischen Milizen trugen im allgemeinen Uniformen, die denen der Berufssoldaten recht ähnlich waren, abgesehen von den Rundhüten, die gewöhnlich die offizielle Kopfbedeckung blieben. Barbados Militia, Light Company, 1805.

G 1st West India Regiment, Gefreiter, ca. 1803–1810 mit dem Ofenrohr-Tschako, der ab 1803 an die westindischen Regimenter ausgegeben wurde. Im gleichen Jahr wurde auch die weiße Ausrüstung genehmigt, doch blieb die schwarze, insofern sie noch diensttüchtig war, oft noch lange Jahre darüber hinaus in Gebrauch. Royal West India Rangers, Hornist, ca. 1810. Diese Einheit trug Grün mit roten Blenden, und die Hornisten hatten enganliegende, kurze Waffenröcke, die mit weißen Litzen mit blauem Zickzack versehen waren. 5th und 8th West India Regiments, Feldwebel, ca. 1808–1812.

H Schwarze Garnisonskompanien, Gefreiter, 1813–6. Altgediente Soldaten der westindischen Regimenter, die zum Garnisonsdienst tauglich waren, wurden in diese beiden Kompanien übersetzt. Im Gegensatz zu den westindischen Regimentern glich der enganliegende, kurze Waffenrock dem der Mannschaften. 2nd West India Regt, Trommler, 1814–1816. Die Trommler der westindischen Regimenter trugen "umgekehrte" Farben verglichen mit der übrigen Armee, in diesem Fall gelb mit roten Blenden. In dieser Epoche trug man "belgische" Tschakos und blaue Gamaschenhosen. Die Embleme auf der Trommel sind denen auf den Regimentsknöpfen nachempfunden. Royal York Rangers, Gefreiter, 1808–1813. Die britischen Kolonialregimenter im Karibik, die aus Europäern rekrutiert wurden, trugen normalerweise die grüne Jacke, die in diesem Fall rote Blenden hat und weiß eingefaßt ist.